STORAGE & SHELVING
THE SHAKER WAY

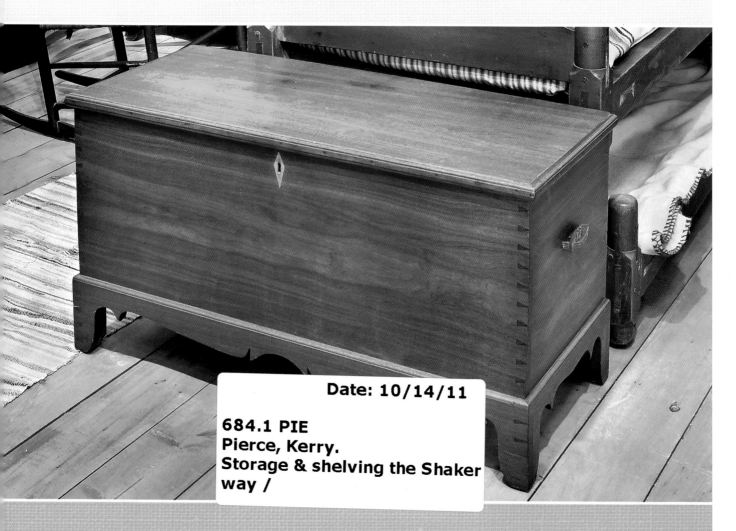

KERRY PIERCE

POPULAR WOODWORKING BOOKS
CINCINNATI, OHIO
www.popularwoodworking.com

Read This Important Safety Notice

To prevent accidents, keep safety in mind while you work. Use the safety guards installed on power equipment; they are for your protection. When working on power equipment, keep fingers away from saw blades, wear safety goggles to prevent injuries from flying wood chips and saw-dust, wear hearing protection and consider installing a dust vacuum to reduce the amount of airborne sawdust in your wood-shop. Don't wear loose clothing, such as neckties or shirts with loose sleeves, or jew-elry, such as rings, necklaces or bracelets, when working on power equipment. Tie back long hair to prevent it from getting caught in your equipment. People who are sensitive to certain chemicals should check the chemical content of any product before using it. The authors and editors who com-piled this book have tried to make the con-tents as accurate and correct as possible. Plans, illustrations, photographs and text have been carefully checked. All instruc-tions, plans and projects should be care-fully read, studied and understood before beginning construction. Due to the variabil-ity of local conditions, construction materi-als, skill levels, etc., neither the author nor Popular Woodworking Books assumes any responsibility for any accidents, injuries, damages or other losses incurred resulting from the material presented in this book. Prices listed for supplies and equipment were current at the time of publication and are subject to change.

Thanks to the Heritage Village Museum at Sharon Woods in Cincinnati, Ohio for letting us use their historal buildings to take some of the project opener photos.

Metric Conversion Chart

to convert	to	multiply by
Inches	Centimeters	2.54
Centimeters	Inches	0.39
Feet	Centimeters	30.48
Centimeters	Feet	0.03
Yards	Meters	0.91
Meters	Yards	1.09

Distributed in Canada by Fraser Direct
100 Armstrong Avenue
Georgetown, Ontario L7G 5S4
Canada

Distributed in the U.K. and Europe by David & Charles
Brunel House
Newton Abbot
Devon TQ12 4PU
England
Tel: (+44) 1626 323200
Fax: (+44) 1626 323319
E-mail: postmaster@davidandcharles.co.uk

Distributed in Australia by Capricorn Link
P.O. Box 704
Windsor, NSW 2756
Australia

Visit our Web site at www.popularwoodworking.com.

Other fine Popular Woodworking Books are available from your local bookstore or direct from the publisher.

13   12   11   10   09   5   4   3   2   1

Library of Congress Cataloging-in-Publication Data

Pierce, Kerry.
  Storage and shelving the Shaker way / by Kerry Pierce. -- 1st ed.
     p. cm.
  Includes index.
  ISBN 978-1-55870-854-9 (pbk. : alk. paper)
  1. Furniture making. 2. Shelving (Furniture) 3. Shaker furniture. I. Ti=
tle.
  TT194.P542 2009
  684.1--dc22

ACQUISITIONS EDITOR: David Thiel
SENIOR EDITOR: Jim Stack
DESIGNER: Brian Roeth
PRODUCTION COORDINATOR: Mark Griffin
PHOTOGRAPHER: Kerry Pierce
ILLUSTRATOR: Kevin Pierce

About the Author

After earning a bachelor's degree in English from Bowling Green State University, and a master's degree in art from Ohio University, Kerry Pierce began a 30-year career as a professional furniture maker. He has specialized in Shaker and Shaker-inspired work for much of that career. Many of his 17 books and 120 magazine articles focus on Shaker woodworking. He has shown his Shaker-inspired work in a number of regional venues. He has served as a contributing Editor of *Woodwork* magazine and is a regular instructor at the Marc Adams School in Indianapolis, teaching most often about Shaker-style chairmaking.

Acknowledgements

As hard as it is to believe, this is the tenth book I've written for the good people at Popular Woodworking Books, and I have come to know some of them well enough to use the term "good people" in its original and specific meaning. They are good people, in particular Jim Stack and David Thiel, who have been both kind and generous, even in situations in which I may not have deserved kindness and generosity.

Thanks, Jim. Thanks, David. It's been a pleasure.

And of course, Elaine, Emily and Andy.

A Word About the Projects

In a perfect world, I would have been able to put my hands on the original model for every piece that appears in this book, but unfortunately project books based on historical originals are rarely written in such a perfect world.

I did manage to physically measure some of the originals I reproduced for this book. Several years ago while visiting the Sabbathday Lake community in Maine, Leonard Brooks permitted me to measure two pieces, one of which is the yellow wood box which appears on page 118. In addition, thanks to the generosity of Larrie Curry, the museum director at Pleasant Hill, I was able to measure the three oval boxes you see on pages 60. On that same trip to Pleasant Hill, I measured the built-ins on the third floor of the Centre Family Dwelling. The drawings my brother, Kevin, prepared from those measurements, are the first measured representations of these magnificent chests of drawers ever published. Likewise, the drawings Kevin did of the Hamlin cupboard on pages 132 are the first measured representations ever published of this important piece. Even if you never choose to build either the built-ins or the Hamlin cupboard, the drawings deserve space on the shelves of any serious student of Shaker furniture. Kevin also measured the walnut blanket chest on page 138, which is among the many fine pieces of Ohio Shaker work in the Warren County Museum in Lebanon, Ohio.

The work you'll find on these pages can be organized into three different categories. First, there is a discussion of the magnificent built-ins on the third floor of the Centre Family Dwelling at Pleasant Hill, Kentucky. I doubt that any reader will construct an exact reproduction of those built-ins, but I think we all can benefit from a study of the measured drawings Kevin prepared of those chests of drawers. What we see there can inform our approaches to built-ins we might construct for our homes. Second, the book includes measured drawings of one large and complex storage piece: The Hamlin cupboard, also from Pleasant Hill. This is a piece an ambitious craftsmen might actually choose to reproduce. But the meat of the book falls into a third category: a number of less imposing pieces, some of which might be constructed by even a relatively inexperienced craftsman. In my presentation of these projects, I decided that I would provide exhaustive photographic documentation for several representative pieces so that a craftsman who might be new to woodworking could be exposed to a set of solutions to all of the technical problems he might face in building such a piece. In the case of the Canterbury chest, that documentation consists of nearly 100 step-by-step photos. Obviously, in a book of only 144 pages, there isn't space for that level of documentation for each of the projects I built for this book, but I think by studying the methods presented in the case of the Canterbury chest, a reader will learn techniques that can be applied to other similar pieces, like the yellow wood box, which is presented with only a handful of photos. In the same way, a reader wishing to build the large shelf unit can find the techniques for doing so in the chapter about the construction of the small shelf unit.

I'm very grateful to the kind people at the Warren County Museum in Ohio, Sabbathday Lake Museum in Maine and the collections at Pleasant Hill, Kentucky for the access they provided us.

The remaining pieces in the book, however, are based on either photos or measured drawings appearing in several sources: John Kassay's *The Book of Shaker Furniture*, John Shea's *Making Authentic Shaker Furniture* and several of Enjer Handberg's drawing books of Shaker furniture.

contents

introduction

THE MATERIAL WORLD OCCUPIED BY 19th-century Shakers was a tidy place in which the accessories of human life — clothing, books, foodstuffs, etc. — were carefully hidden away in containers designed for their orderly storage. Sewing notions were stowed away in sewing baskets or sewing chests like the adapted chest appearing on page 74. Miscellaneous household goods were often stored in any of dozens of different types of oval boxes and carriers, like those you'll find on page 60. Candles were stored in many different kinds of nailed or dovetailed candle boxes. The ubiquitous Shaker peg rail found on the walls of nearly every room in every Shaker dwelling was designed as a long-term anchoring system for a variety of cupboards, sconces, hangers, as well as a short-term anchoring system for chairs and other furniture miscellanea so that floors could be swept more easily. A discussion of peg rails, as well as measured drawings and step-by-step construction details for storage units designed to be hung from these rails can be found on page 20.

In addition, the Shakers excelled in the ingenious construction of a variety of free-standing cupboards and cabinets not quite like those designed in the World. Consider the many sewing desks and tables built in Shaker communities. Similar constructions built in the World, had drawers opening on only one face of the cabinet (the front face), but in the Shaker Universe, because Sisters often worked in groups surrounding a central sewing table or cabinet, the drawers opened on two, three or four sides. This ingenious approach to storage problem solving was common throughout the Shaker Universe.

The Shakers also excelled in the design and construction of more straight-forward free-standing storage units, like the Hamlin cupboard which appears on page 132. The three doors and four drawers of this magnificent construction all open on the same face of the cupboard, but, because of its scale and meticulously detailed composition, the piece is no less arresting visually than the more atypically designed sewing desks.

Finally, the population of 19th-century Shakers included some of the pre-eminent American designers of built-in furniture. Every Shaker community I've ever visited includes

some storage furniture built into closets, under stairways or into the unused ends of hallways. The magnificent U-shaped built-ins, on the third floor of the Centre-Family Dwelling at Pleasant Hill, Kentucky, is my favorite among these. Measured drawings of that construction appear on pages 10-11.

Unlike the Amish — to which they're often mistakenly compared — the Shakers were remarkably forward thinking, embracing, and in some cases, creating new technologies to help them in their many agrarian and manufacturing efforts. The circular saw, for example, is often identified as the product of an imaginative Shaker Sister, and while that story may or may not be true, there is no doubt that the Shakers were among the very first to make widespread use of this revolutionary tool. They were similarly forward thinking in their approach to storage furniture and woodenware. Recently, in one of our local home improvement stores, I walked past a display touting a new storage system which consisted of a series of long rails which could be screwed to the wall of perhaps a garage or a utility room, and then a variety of hooks and pegs could be

snapped into this rail so that it could used to hold all kinds of household goods in an effort to bring order to cluttered rooms. Not exactly new, I thought. Two hundred years ago, the Shakers were using the same system — the peg rail system — to bring order to their lives.

If you're looking for imaginative solutions to contemporary storage problems, I think you'll find what you're looking for here on the pages of this book. In most cases, I present the objects in their original forms, but in others, I present them with alterations that might make better sense for a contemporary home. For example, hand sewing was practiced in every 19th-century Shaker community. As a result, the Shakers produced an astonishing variety of sewing desks, tables, chest, cabinets and cupboards. The sewing chest I present here I offer with modifications that would convert it to a large jewelry chest.

PROJECT ONE

CENTRE FAMILY DWELLING BUILT-INS

In the 19th century, American storage notions shifted, placing less emphasis on free-standing storage furniture and more emphasis on built-in storage furniture, and the designer/craftsmen of the country's many Shaker communities were among the leading exponents of this new emphasis. That the Shakers would be on the forefront in the realm of built-in storage furniture is hardly surprising because, unlike families in the World who might retain a residence for only a generation (or even a part of a generation), Shaker families typically inhabited the same dwelling for many generations, making portable storage furniture much less necessary.

My favorite Shaker built-ins are those on the third floor of the Centre Family Dwelling at Pleasant Hill, Kentucky. These chests-of-drawers are monuments to the design and woodworking skills of the Shaker craftsmen who created them. The 45 oversized drawers (each almost three feet long and eight inches high) likely provided storage for the goods (perhaps the seasonal clothing) of the nearly 100 residents who once made their home in the Centre Family Dwelling. Because these storage units were placed directly underneath a large skylight cut into the roof of the dwelling, residents could search the contents of the drawers without resorting to candles or lamps.

Unfortunately, we know nothing about the history of these magnificent built-ins. The staff of Pleasant Hill has not found a single scrap of documentary evidence related to the design, construction or purpose of the units. The architectural drawings, prepared by Pleasant Hill resident Micajah Burnett, to guide the construction of the Centre Family Dwelling and its many installations, are long gone.

In the case of these third-floor built-ins, we know only what we see.

By definition, built-ins are designed to fit specific spaces. Benches and a table for a kitchen breakfast nook are designed to fill a kitchen alcove. In the same way, an entertainment center is designed to occupy the full width of one end of a family room. The enormous storage unit pictured here was designed to occupy a particular architectural space in one end of the hallway at the top of the third-floor stairway in the Centre Family Dwelling. It's unlikely that anyone would ever wish to reproduce this array of chests of drawers, but there is much that we can learn about the process of creating built-in furniture by studying the way these cabinets were constructed.

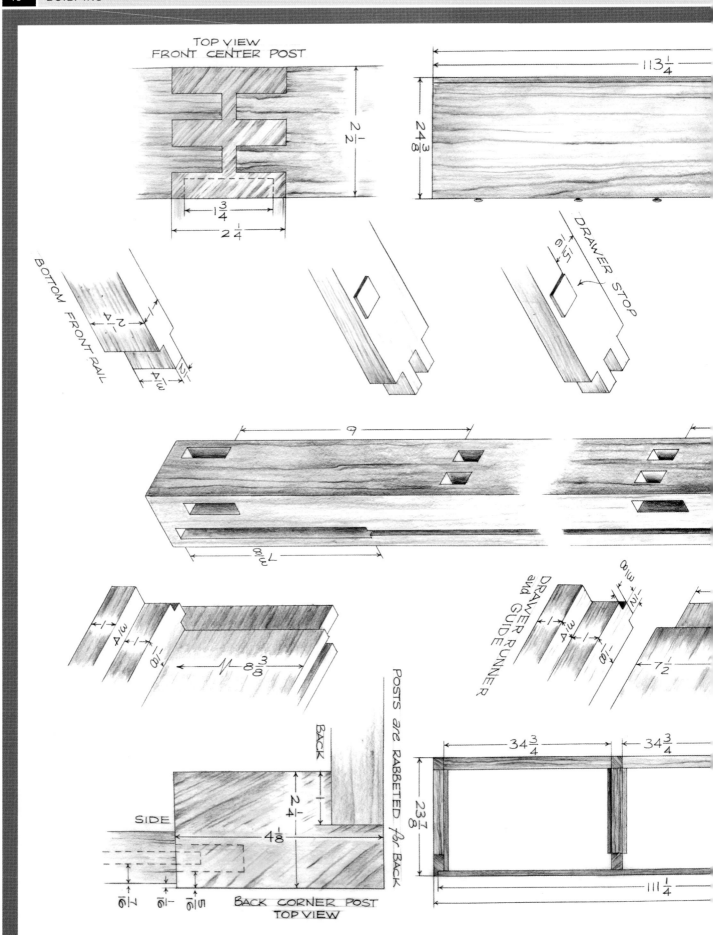

TOP VIEW
FRONT CENTER POST

$2\frac{1}{2}$

$1\frac{3}{4}$

$2\frac{1}{4}$

$113\frac{1}{4}$

$24\frac{3}{8}$

BOTTOM FRONT RAIL

$2\frac{1}{4}$

$\frac{3}{4}$

$\frac{5}{16}$

DRAWER STOP

9

$1\frac{3}{8}$

$\frac{3}{4}$

1

$1\frac{1}{8}$

$8\frac{3}{8}$

DRAWER RUNNER
and GUIDE

$\frac{3}{8}$

$\frac{1}{2}$

$\frac{3}{4}$

1

$1\frac{1}{8}$

$7\frac{1}{2}$

BACK

$2\frac{1}{4}$

SIDE

$4\frac{1}{8}$

$\frac{7}{16}$ $\frac{1}{16}$ $\frac{5}{16}$

BACK CORNER POST
TOP VIEW

POSTS are RABBETED for BACK

$34\frac{3}{4}$ $34\frac{3}{4}$

$23\frac{7}{8}$

$111\frac{1}{4}$

TOP VIEW

FRONT VIEW

TOP FRONT RAIL

FRONT CORNER POST

SIDE RAIL

$137\frac{5}{8}$

$24\frac{3}{8}$

$23\frac{7}{8}$

$113\frac{1}{4}$

$113\frac{1}{4}$

$34\frac{3}{4}$

8

$6\frac{1}{2}$

$4\frac{1}{8}$

$17\frac{1}{4}$

$2\frac{1}{2}$

$2\frac{1}{4}$

$34\frac{3}{4}$

$2\frac{1}{4}$

$34\frac{3}{4}$

$2\frac{1}{4}$

$34\frac{3}{4}$

$2\frac{1}{4}$

$2\frac{1}{2}$

$2\frac{1}{4}$

$17\frac{1}{4}$

$23\frac{7}{8}$

$4\frac{1}{8}$

161

$8\frac{3}{8}$

$32\frac{3}{8}$

$7\frac{1}{2}$

$49\frac{1}{4}$

SITING

It's possible to argue that these built-ins were included in Micajah Burnett's original design, based on their location and the enormous amount of natural light that location was designed to receive.

Without something of the scale of these built-ins, this particular large space would have been unused, and there is no other space of this size that was not put to some purpose in the Centre Family Dwelling. That fact alone argues for these units being included in the original design of the building. In addition, the spectacular use of natural light entering the building through the skylights above these units, illuminating the drawers and their contents, also argues for the existence of something of substantial size and complexity in this location from the earliest days of Burnett's planning of the dwelling.

The only detail in the environment of the built-ins that suggests these constructions were not original equipment is the floor discontinuity that appears halfway between the stairways leading to the third floor and the built-ins (photo No.1). The flooring underneath the built-ins is about half the width of the flooring around the stairways, which suggests it was cut from a different stock of material, probably at a later time than the flooring surrounding the stairway. In fact, given the high degree of organization we see elsewhere in the Centre Family Dwelling, the floor discontinuity is very suggestive. It's difficult to imagine a situation during the original construction of the Centre Family Dwelling in which the flooring of two different but adjacent areas would have been installed at the same approximate time but of completely different and unconnected materials. We see, for example, no boards from the stairway area continuing into the built-in area. Instead we see a clear line of demarcation separating the two, and this line argues in favor of ascribing the flooring to two different dates, with the flooring around the stairways being original equipment and the flooring underneath the built-ins installed at the same time as the built-ins.

There is one other provocative siting detail, and that is the presence of a large column of unused and enclosed space at either end of the central section of drawer stacks. These spaces are boxed off equal in width and length to the depths of the adjacent drawers.

These spaces are bounded on the outside by the walls, on the inside by the walls of the built-ins which support the drawer runners, on the bottom by the floor of the space, and on the top by the top of the built-ins.

It's fun to think that these two spaces, each of which is large enough to conceal a crouched man, might have been created as hiding places for something of historical importance (like Micajah Burnett's missing drawings of the Centre Family Dwelling). But the truth is that, unlike modern architects who labor to make use of every inch of a building's interior space, architects of Burnett's era simply built to a different standard — one that reflected the seemingly infinite real estate and material available to builders of the era. In other words, if a building's most efficient design included some walled off and therefore unused spaces large enough to be put to use, so be it.

DESIGN

One of the most powerful elements of the Shaker aesthetic is the straight-forward relationship between form and function, and that relationship is never more evident than it is here in this series of built-ins.

The designer of the Centre Family built-ins was assigned the task of creating storage for a large number of items small enough to be packed into drawers. The most natural and direct response to that design assignment would be to create a series of identical units with a large number of equal-size drawers. That approach to the design problem not only reflects the Shaker belief in the sublimation of individuality in favor of community, it also provides a design context for a piece with a powerful visual rhythm. Imagine how much less visual impact this storage area would have had if it had been filled with a number of individually designed three- or four-drawer chests holding 45 large drawers. The storage capacity of the area would have been the same, but these individually designed units would have lacked the aesthetic presence achieved by the stately repetition of equal shapes.

Cherry was the preferred primary wood for Pleasant Hill casework throughout the community's history, appearing far more often in this context than any other species. Walnut is seen but usually in smaller, less significant pieces, and maple is found as a primary wood even more rarely than walnut. In particular, the cabinetmakers of Pleasant Hill favored the relatively rare curly variant of cherry. The magnificent Pleasant Hill secretary now displayed in one of the second floor rooms of the meetinghouse was executed in curly cherry, and we see that same variant here in the drawer fronts of the third-floor built-ins.

This marriage of extremely simple Shaker forms and figured material is often cited by connoisseurs of Shaker work with good reason. Figured material is seen to best advantage on surfaces not modified by carving or veneering, which can distract the eye from the material itself. The unadorned components of Shaker work provide a perfect context for the appreciation of figured material.

1 After climbing up three very long flights of stairs to reach the third floor of the Centre Family Dwelling at Pleasant Hill, Kentucky, you see this magnificent array of drawer stacks executed in curly cherry. It's a powerful moment for any admirer of Shaker furniture.

Such is the case with these built-ins. Each drawer front is a simple, unadorned rectangle, with no moulded edges, no applied cock bead, not even the scratch-stock, simulated cock bead found on many other Pleasant Hill drawer fronts. The posts and drawer rails appear as simple, although long, rectangles. The tops of the built-ins are glued-up panels that were planed flat, installed with a slight overhang and without edge treatment. The posts and rails that separate the drawers are also simple rectangles. There is no moulding at the base of the units to smooth the transition with the floor. While there is a narrow strip running the full length of the units where the top meets the wall, this strip is just a narrow rip without embellishment.

In fact, I think it's possible to argue that this strip was not part of the original design, being added sometime after the installation of the built-ins. The hundreds of meticulously cut dovetail sockets on the drawers of these units demonstrate a very high level of craftsmanship, and I'm reluctant to believe that such an accomplished craftsman (or craftsmen) would have relied on something as clumsy as this strip to conceal gaps between the back

edge of the top and the wall. My guess is that the top was originally scribed and fit to the wall. Then, over a period of years as the building settled, slight gaps appeared between the back edge and the wall. It's my guess that at that time the strip was added to cover the gap.

Only the turned wooden knobs offer any detail that transcends simple function. These knobs sit on the drawer fronts on shallow half beads, which, strictly speaking, are unnecessary since plain coves under the knobs' mushroom caps would permit fingers to grasp the knobs and open the drawers.

It would be interesting to know the history of these knobs. Were they turned by Shaker craftsmen perhaps in large numbers and then selected for these drawers? Were they purchased from a supplier in the World? Or, were they designed specifically for the drawers of these built-ins?

CONSTRUCTION

Photo No.10 reveals the construction details of the cases. The ends employ post-and-panel construction which is

2 Although the drawers are essentially the same size, each one is custom fit to its opening.

typical of most Pleasant Hill chests of drawers. The wide rails at the top and bottom are tenoned into the posts. A large panel, planed thin, floats in grooves plowed on the inside edges of the posts and rails. This construction is still today favored for solid-wood end panels because it allows a wide central panel to shrink without cracking any of the end panel's components. The drawer rails across the front of the units are tenoned on each end into the posts. The drawer runners (which carry the weight of the drawers) and the drawer guides are then tenoned and/or nailed to the posts.

The drawer stops, which can be seen in photo No.11, are thin strips of wood glued to the tops of the drawer rails. When the back side of the drawer front strikes these little strips of wood, the drawer is in the fully-closed position.

The drawers themselves are assembled with half-blind dovetails in the front and through dovetails in the back — all very conventional — except for one detail: Whereas the dovetails are cut on the drawer sides at the front of the drawers, the dovetails on the back of the drawers are cut on the backs of the drawers. This sounds a little confusing, but if you look at photos No.5 and No.6, I think you can see what I'm talking about. In the drawer on the right side of No.5, you can see an entire drawer side showing

tails at the top and pins at the bottom. Then in No.6, you see a more detailed view of the joinery at the back of the drawer. The piece on the left-hand side of the drawer is the drawer back. Notice that the tails are cut on that piece while the matching pins are cut on the side of the drawer, the part that runs across the top of that photo.

Although I have seen this method of construction before, it is unusual. Typically, the dovetails at the front and back of the drawer are cut on the drawer sides, with the pins being cut on the drawer front and the drawer back.

This non-standard method of construction may have been an attempt to put in place a mechanical resistance to separation in both directions, instead of simply in the front-to-back direction. This non-standard method, however, doesn't fit the with the forces drawer joinery is required to withstand. When you open a drawer, the force is directed from front to back. There is very little lateral force a drawer's components need to withstand.

There are two other drawer construction details I would like to point out, both of which are problematic.

First, the drawer bottoms are fit into grooves on the inside of the drawer sides and the back face of the drawer front. This is standard, first-quality construction. However, instead of attaching the drawer bottom to the

3, 4 The half-blind dovetails at the front of each drawer required the chopping of a total of 540 sockets for each of the 540 dovetails, and — as you can see here — the quality of the workmanship is excellent, an excellence maintained throughout the entire run of drawers.

bottom of the drawer back with a screw housed in a notch cut in the drawer bottom (as you can see in the Canterbury chest, page 110, step 66), the drawer bottom is simply nailed to the bottom edge of the drawer back (photo No.6). The problem with this method (which I admit I used for years) is that if the drawer bottom shrinks across its width enough to pull out of the groove on the back side of the drawer front, the drawer bottom can't be repositioned without first digging the nail head out of the wood of the drawer bottom. When the drawer bottom is held in place with a screw in a notch on the drawer bottom, the screw can be loosened, the drawer bottom slid back into the groove on the back of the drawer front, and the screw retightened. Much simpler.

5 Traditionally, the dovetails at the front and at the back of a drawer are cut on the drawer sides. The mating pins are then cut on the drawer front and the drawer back. These drawers, however, vary from that tradition. Looking at the drawer on the right side, you'll see there are tails at the front end of the drawer side and pins on the back end of that same drawer side—pins which mate up with the tails that were cut on the end of the drawer back. Notice, also, the liberal use of glue blocks to provide support for the drawer bottom.

A second, even more problematic, issue can be seen in photo No.6. The positioning of the drawer bottom is re-enforced through the use of glue blocks. If the glue blocks had been glued only on the edge that mates with the drawer side, the blocks could have supported the bottom without negative consequences. However, the glue blocks were glued on both the surface that mates with the drawer side as well as the surface that mates with the drawer bottom. Because the drawer bottom wasn't free to slide in its grooves a crack opened up just to the right of the glue block.

SIMPLEST FORMS

While this collection of built-ins would be striking in any setting, it is particularly potent here, washed in strong natural light from above and nestled within the embrace of three white-painted walls. It is a fit reward for those visitors who have made the arduous climb up three very long flights of stairs, who turn around the newel post at the top of that last flight and who lift their eyes to the other end of the landing to see this revelation in curly cherry which stands as a joyous reminder to all of us who work in wood that it is possible to infuse the simplest forms with great meaning when those forms are executed by highly skilled craftsmen intensely committed to the task before them.

Side

Back

6 This close-up of the rear corner of one of the drawers shows the tails on one end of the drawer back and the matching pins on the drawer side. The crack in the drawer bottom is likely a result of the fact that the glue blocks are glued to both the drawer bottom and the drawer side, which prevents the drawer bottom from sliding in the grooves as it shrinks across its width. Note the nail in the bottom panel securing it to the drawer back.

7 This close-up of one set of dovetails indicates the precision with which these dovetails were cut.

8 The knobs are the only design element of the built-ins that reveal any detail that is not strictly functional: the little half bead at the base of the knob.

9 Each of the 45 drawers is custom fit to its opening, and the drawer and matching opening are identified by numbers stamped on each. In this picture you can see a number stamped on the end grain of a dovetail pin.

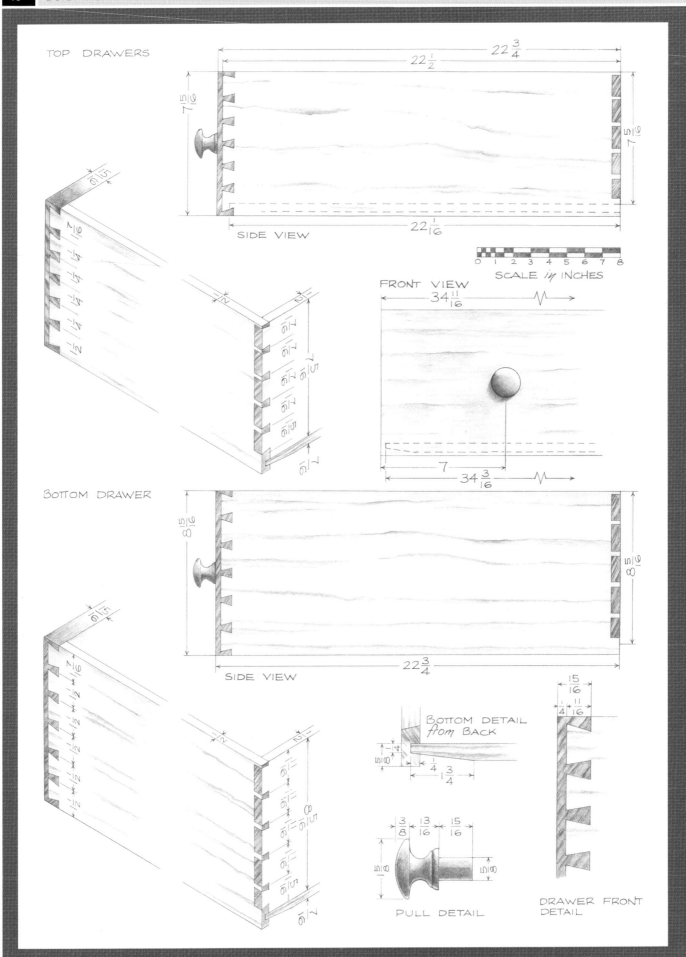

TOP DRAWERS

$22\frac{3}{4}$

$22\frac{1}{2}$

$7\frac{15}{16}$

$7\frac{5}{16}$

$22\frac{1}{16}$

SIDE VIEW

$\frac{15}{16}$

$7\frac{1}{16}$

$1\frac{1}{4}$

$1\frac{1}{4}$

$1\frac{1}{4}$

$1\frac{1}{2}$

$\frac{1}{2}$

$\frac{1}{2}$

$1\frac{1}{16}$

$1\frac{1}{16}$

$1\frac{1}{16}$

$1\frac{5}{16}$

$7\frac{5}{16}$

$1\frac{1}{16}$

0 1 2 3 4 5 6 7 8

SCALE in INCHES

FRONT VIEW

$34\frac{11}{16}$

7

$34\frac{3}{16}$

BOTTOM DRAWER

$8\frac{15}{16}$

$8\frac{5}{16}$

$22\frac{3}{4}$

SIDE VIEW

$\frac{15}{16}$

$8\frac{7}{16}$

$\frac{1}{2}$

$\frac{1}{2}$

$\frac{1}{2}$

$\frac{1}{2}$

$\frac{1}{2}$

$\frac{1}{2}$

$1\frac{1}{16}$

$1\frac{1}{16}$

$1\frac{1}{16}$

$1\frac{1}{16}$

$1\frac{5}{16}$

$8\frac{5}{16}$

$\frac{1}{2}$

BOTTOM DETAIL
from BACK

$1\frac{1}{4}$

$\frac{5}{8}$

$\frac{1}{4}$

$1\frac{3}{4}$

$\frac{3}{8}$

$\frac{13}{16}$

$\frac{15}{16}$

$1\frac{1}{8}$

$1\frac{5}{8}$

PULL DETAIL

$\frac{15}{16}$

$\frac{1}{4}$

$\frac{11}{16}$

DRAWER FRONT
DETAIL

10 This unit—like virtually all of the chests of drawers at Pleasant Hill—was constructed using the post-and-panel method to fabricate the end panels. The wide top and bottom rails of those end panels are tenoned into the posts. The large central panel is planed thin and rides, unglued, in grooves plowed on the inside edges of the posts and the two rails. This construction method allows the large floating panel to expand and contract across its width without causing any cracking.

11 The little strips of wood glued to the drawer rails are the drawer stops. When the back side of the drawer front strikes these strips, the drawers are fully closed.

The Peg/Rail System

PROJECT ONE

THE PEG/RAIL STORAGE SYSTEM

Few 19th century American buildings were completely without pegs or hooks on their walls. These simple devices were
used to keep coats off the floor or as a means of organiz-
ing tools, coils of rope and wire — in general as a means of
keeping clutter up out of the way so the floor could be used
for other purposes.

But only the Shakers institutionalized the use of peg rails,
requiring that they be used just about everywhere there was
sufficient wall space to mount them.

Ann Lee, the founder of the religion commonly known
as the Shakers (formally known as the United Society of
Believers in the First and Second Appearance of Christ (Ann
Lee, of course, was the second appearance) demanded of
her followers that they be scrupulous about keeping their
living quarters and communal areas free of dust and grime.
To facilitate the regular sweeping this demand required, the
Shakers modified their living environment. For instance, in
many of the communities, the dining chairs were made with
low two-slat backs so that they could be pushed completely
under the dining tables in order to make it easier to sweep
the floor. The omnipresent peg rails performed a similar
function. When it was time to sweep a room, much of the
room's furniture, including the chairs, would be hung on
peg rails, clearing the room.

1 In this photo of the second floor infirmary in the Centre Family Dwelling at
Pleasant Hill, Kentucky, pegs are used in two different locations. First, a small poplar cupboard is hanging from two pegs on the rail that encircles the room. Second,
there are two more pegs on the side of the little dry sink.

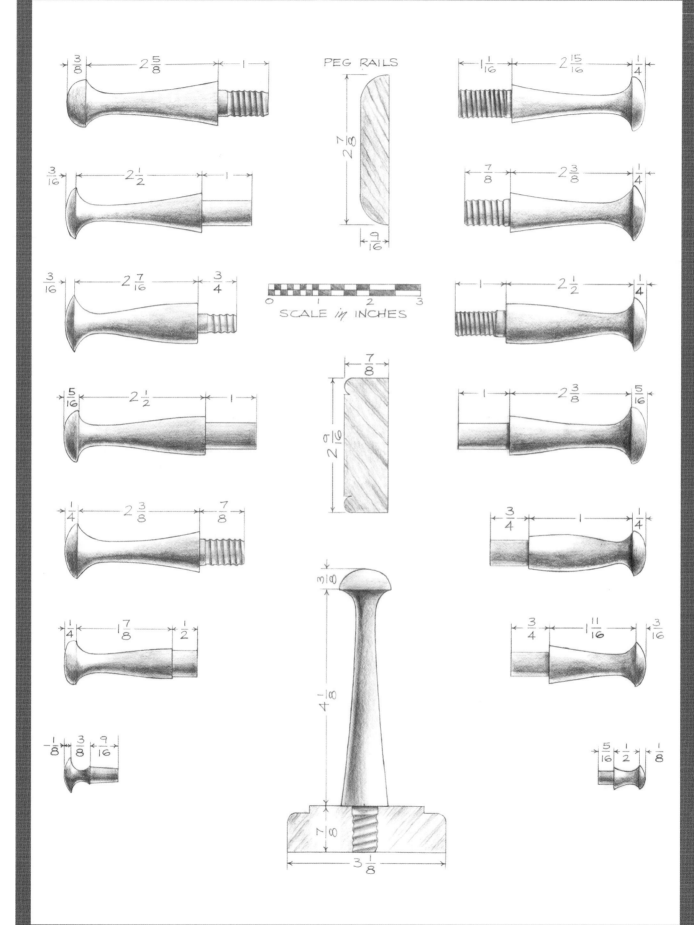

PEG RAILS

SCALE *in* INCHES

2 This room on the second floor of the Meeting House at Pleasant Hill, Kentucky, has two peg rails: one at head height and the other at the approximate upper limit of a resident's reach.

3 Shakers often hung their clothing from wooden hangers which were suspended on leather straps slung over pegs. This rare triple hanger is displayed in one of the first floor rooms in the Centre Family Dwelling at Pleasant Hill.

4 There was considerable variation in the way pegs were spaced. The photo of the infirmary on page 20 shows pegs spaced approximately 13" apart. The pegs shown here, from the second floor of the Meeting House, are about half that spacing.

PROJECT TWO

HANGING CUPBOARD

Shakers used their peg rails, and occasonally nails and screws, as temporary mooring points for things they wanted off the floor to make sweeping easier. They also used the peg rails as permanent or semi-permanent mooring points for a variety of pieces specifically designed to be hung from the pegs on these rails: candle sconces, shelving units, clothes hangers, key and match holders, and so on. Among these pieces were a number of utility cupboards that could be hung from the pegs. Then — as a community's changing needs might require — these cupboards could be taken from one room to another or one building to another to be hung on pegs in the new location.

The original of this simple little cupboard was made in the New Lebanon community early in the 19th century. It's a piece I've admired since I first spotted it in John Kassay's *The Book of Shaker Furniture*. However, I've never had the opportunity to measure the cupboard. The reproduction you see here was scaled up from a small photo in Kassay's book.

Although I didn't have a chance to personally examine this particular cupboard, I have measured other Shaker cupboards of this type, and my method of construction followed the methods I saw in the cases of those other cupboards. Specifically, I built a box of fairly thick material, then added a false top and false bottom of thin-

ner material which imparts an impression of lightness to the finished piece.

A word about the material I used in building this piece. Twenty-five years ago, my dad, who, like me, is a bit of a wood collector, gave me a half dozen short pieces of wormy Spanish cedar he'd picked up at a sawmill. I think the gift was inspired by some comments I had made about someday building a humidor, and Spanish cedar is frequently used to line the interiors of humidors. The humidor never materialized, and the wood sat in my wood storage room for several years until I was picking out material for the pieces in this book, I found the cedar and had just enough material for this cupboard.

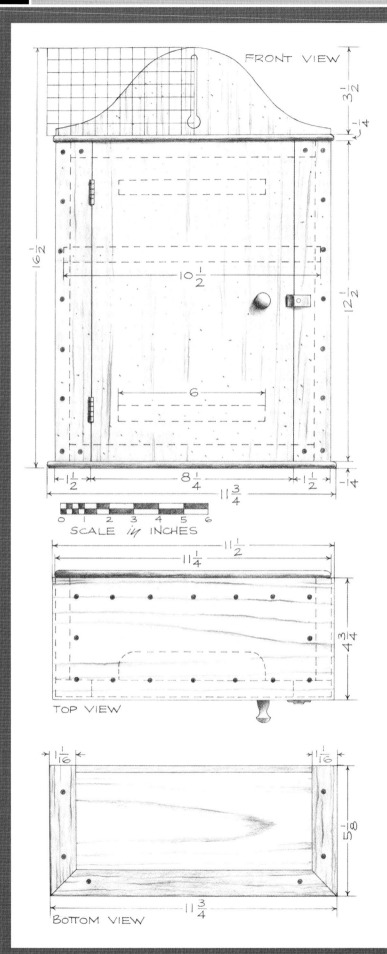

FRONT VIEW

$3\frac{1}{2}$

$\frac{1}{4}$

$16\frac{1}{2}$

$10\frac{1}{2}$

$12\frac{1}{2}$

6

$1\frac{1}{2}$ $8\frac{1}{4}$ $1\frac{1}{2}$ $\frac{1}{4}$

$11\frac{3}{4}$

SCALE in INCHES

0 1 2 3 4 5 6

TOP VIEW

$11\frac{1}{2}$

$11\frac{1}{4}$

$4\frac{3}{4}$

BOTTOM VIEW

$1\frac{1}{16}$ $1\frac{1}{16}$

$5\frac{1}{8}$

$11\frac{3}{4}$

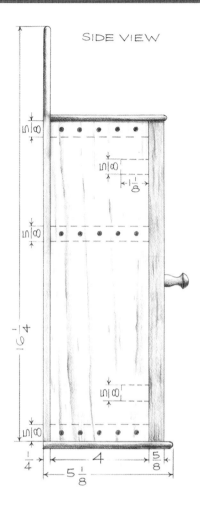

SIDE VIEW

$\frac{5}{8}$

$\frac{5}{8}$

$1\frac{1}{8}$

$\frac{5}{8}$

$16\frac{1}{4}$

$\frac{5}{8}$

$\frac{5}{8}$

$\frac{1}{4}$ 4 $\frac{5}{8}$

$5\frac{1}{8}$

KNOB DETAIL

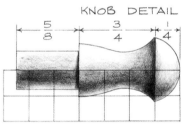

$\frac{5}{8}$ $\frac{3}{4}$ $\frac{1}{4}$

EACH GRID SQUARE
REPRESENTS $\frac{1}{4}$ INCH

$\frac{1}{4}$

LATCH DETAIL

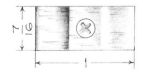

$\frac{7}{16}$

1

1 One of the reasons I picked wormy Spanish cedar for this cupboard was my hope that the heads of the nails I used to assemble the piece (the original was also nailed together) would be less noticeable on surfaces scattered with dark wormholes. I selected the boards with the heaviest spotting of worm holes for the front and back. The other pieces I used to form the top, sides and bottom of the cupboard.

2 Before I edge-jointed the boards, I checked the tables on my jointer to verify that they were square with the fence.

3 When you're using a jointer to square up an edge, you start with downward force on the infeed table with your left hand and push the board forward over the jointer knives with your right hand. I begin by flattening the concave edge of a board so that I've got material on both ends of the board I can stabilize against my jointer tables.

4 As you move the board across the knives, you transfer your downward pressure to the outfeed table. Remember to keep the board tight against the fence throughout the jointing process.

5 After jointing the edge with a machine, I took a single shaving from that edge with a jointing plane, in this case an antique Stanley No.7. This finishing touch removes the faint ripples left behind by the machine jointer. I know you can glue up good panels without this last jointing step, but I think this step adds an extra measure of precision to the jointed edge, so it has become a regular part of my jointing method.

6 In order to check the quality of the joints, I perform two checks with the loose boards stacked on edge while the bottom board is secured in a vise. The first check is a visual check to see that there aren't any light gaps in any of the joints.

7 The second check requires a straight edge. I simply place the straight edge against the stack of boards to make sure that the faces of these boards all lay in the same plane.

8 After a dry fit to get all my clamps and cauls into the right positions, I apply a bead of glue to each surface to be joined and then spread the glue with a flat stick as shown here.

9 I raise the panel being glued on cleats to place it in line with the pressure points of the clamps. I then add cauls to the top surface of the panel to ensure that the panel will dry flat. Here, I'm checking the flatness of the clamped panel with the blade of a framing square.

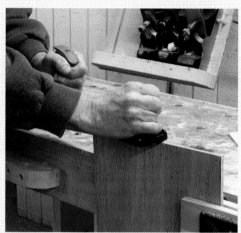

10 After thicknessing the stock for the back, I laid my pattern on that stock and traced the shape of the back. I then cut out that shape on my band saw.

11 I cleaned up the saw marks on the bottom and the two sides with a hand plane.

12 The top of the back has a slight radius which I fashioned with hand tools. First, I did some marking with a pencil to establish the limits of that radius.

13 With a rasp, I connected the pencil line in the center of the edge with the lines on the front and back.

14 The keyhole slot on the back is round at the top and at the bottom. I established those rounds with Forstner bits.

15 I then cut the rest of the slot with a saber saw.

16 I finished the slot with a little rasp work.

17 I next ripped off the two side pieces for the cupboard front.

18 Kassay's notes about the original indicate a shelf. I decided to house the ends of that shelf in a pair of dadoes which I cut with repeated passes on my radial arm saw.

20 Before I nail anything together, I lay out and predrill the through holes.

19 Like almost every other branch of the woodworking tree, a simple procedure like nailing can become quite complicated if you look at it deeply enough.

Although I used period-appropriate cut nails for the Canterbury chest appearing elsewhere in this book, I choose a different kind of fastener for this little cupboard because the Spanish cedar is a bit brittle and I was afraid that the taper in the shank of a cut nail might cause splitting problems, even if I pre-drilled holes. I opted then to use 4d coated box nails.

Box nails have untapered shanks and blunted ends, two characteristics that reduce the likelihood of splitting the material in which they're driven, and, at $1^1/_2$" in length, I felt they were of sufficient size to hold the components together, particularly if I selected the coated variety of box nail.

Nails can be coated with several different compounds. For example, many nails destined for exterior use, are galvanized with a zinc coating to protect the nail from degrading when exposed to the elements. The coating I selected is a resin coating (a dusty greenish-brown material) that doesn't increase the diameter of the nail the way a zinc coating does but nevertheless provides the nail with enormous gripping power.

Before I selected the size nails I would use, I experimented with several sizes on scrap as shown here. I also experimented with several different drill bits before choosing one that matched up with 4d box nails. The hole should be drilled only through the top board, and the diameter of the hole should be slightly less than the diameter of the nail shank.

21 Protecting the bottom of the cupboard with a length of scrap material, I nailed the cupboard's frame together.

22 I purposely left the back slightly oversized so I would have material to plane down in order to achieve a good fit.

23 I decided to hinge the door before I installed the frame components. Here, I'm cutting the mortise on the frame component from which the door would hang.

24 After nibbling away the bulk of the waste, I pared the hinge mortise flat.

25 Center punches, like the one I'm holding here, simplify the process of accurately locating screw holes for hinges. The blunt point of the punch fills the hinge's screw hole and the steeply tapered tip then locates the exact center of that screw hole and marks that center with a shallow depression. (I have several different sizes of center punches, each one suitable for specific-size screw holes.)

26 After the hinges have been installed on the door frame, I marked the hinge location on the door.

27 After I'd nailed the two door frame components in place, I did a final fitting of the door to its opening using a block plane.

28 This detail shot shows the bottom of the door and the adjacent frame component. Notice that the edge of the door is planed at an angle. This is necessary because—as the door opens—the bottom corner of that edge will collide with the frame component if the door edge isn't either given a bevel or planed with a wide gap.

29 I had also left the door frame components wide enough to give me material to plane down after they'd been installed.

30 The knob for the cupboard's door is quite small. I formed the $^3/_8$" tenon with a butt chisel laid bevel side down on my tool rest.

31 I shaped the cove of the knob with a $^1/_4$" fingernail gouge as shown. Then, using a skew chisel as shown in Photo 38 on page 84, I finished off the top of the knob with several paring cuts.

32 It is impossible to safely shape a tiny form like the latch of this cupboard using a band saw—unless you first do a little planning. I cut the latch from this scrap of walnut, laying out the form on one end of the scrap and using the other end to move the cut lines into the saw blade.

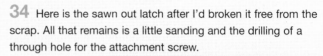

33 This is the final cut the latch requires. Instead of making a through cut—which might result in the tiny part flying across the shop—I stopped this final cut when there was still a tiny hinge of wood attaching the latch to the larger piece of scrap. I then broke off the hinge.

34 Here is the sawn out latch after I'd broken it free from the scrap. All that remains is a little sanding and the drilling of a through hole for the attachment screw.

35 Although I doubt the original cupboard had them, I added a pair of cleats to the back of the door to offer some resistance to the cupping that inevitably occurs in a wide piece of unsupported solid wood.

36 When I said I had just enough material for this cupboard, I wasn't being quite honest. After assembling the cupboard, I didn't have any material for the false bottom. But I did have some narrow strips, ripped from other parts of the cupboard. I decided to attach this three-piece mitered frame to the bottom of the cupboard, which gives the appearance of a complete false bottom.

PROJECT THREE

CURLY-MAPLE HANGING SHELF

The original on which this reproduction is based was made in Hancock, Massachusetts. It is now in the collection of the Hancock Shaker Village there. It was designed to be suspended from a cord run between the $1/4$" holes drilled in the ends, a cord which was positioned over a pair of pegs.

Mine is very similar to the original with the exception of joinery. I added a number of $1^1/4$" coarse-threaded drywall screws that pass through the dadoed ends of the shelves for a little extra strength. The heads of the screws are countersunk and concealed under maple plugs planed flush.

These plugs are available from many dealers in two forms, both of which are tapered on the sides to permit them to be tapped into holes and achieve tight fits. Some are cut from end grain stock and so match up well in such an application. Others, like the plugs I used on this piece, are cut from side grain and match up better in holes drilled in side-grain stock.

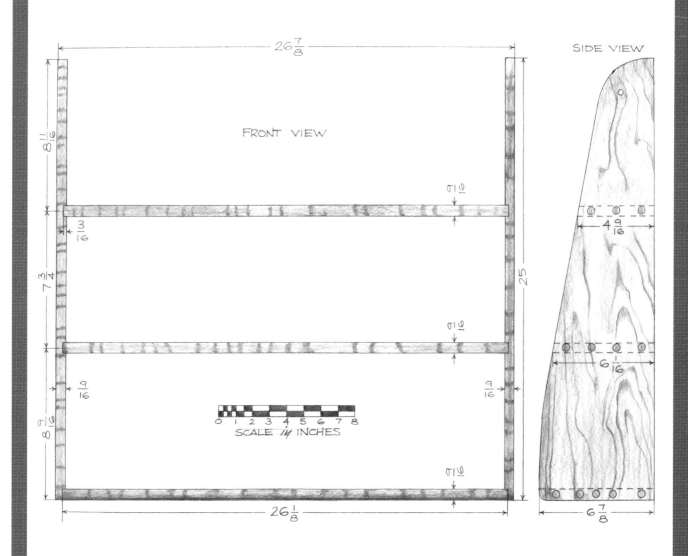

FRONT VIEW

$26\frac{7}{8}$

$8\frac{11}{16}$

$\frac{3}{16}$

$7\frac{3}{4}$

$\frac{9}{16}$

$8\frac{9}{16}$

$\frac{9}{16}$

$\frac{9}{16}$

$\frac{9}{16}$

$\frac{9}{16}$

$\frac{9}{16}$

25

$26\frac{1}{8}$

0 1 2 3 4 5 6 7 8
SCALE IN INCHES

SIDE VIEW

$4\frac{9}{16}$

$6\frac{11}{16}$

$6\frac{7}{8}$

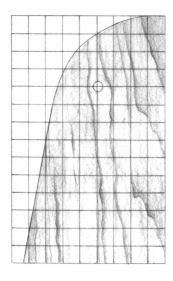

EACH GRID SQUARE
REPRESENTS $\frac{1}{2}$ INCH

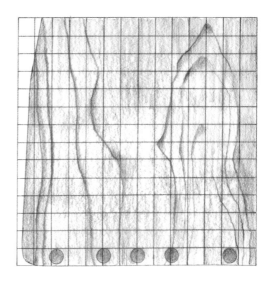

1 I've never done any polling on the subject, but my experience—informed by profiling over 50 furniture makers for books and magazines—is that most craftsmen rely on 6"-8" jointers to flatten stock before running it through a thickness planer. The wider commercial-grade machines we might wish to own can carry price tags greater than the total price of all our other woodworking machinery. This means that we are often confronted with this problem: How do we flatten boards too wide for the head on our relatively narrow jointers?

2 One option, which I frequently exercise in the case of particularly fine, wide boards, is the use of hand planes, but there is another way to handle such material: Saw it in half and after surfacing it, rejoin the halves.

3 It's a simple matter to flatten the two halves.

4 When you're flattening the two halves on your jointer, it isn't necessary to produce surfaces completely without saw marks. All that's needed are surfaces that are generally in the same plane like these shown here.

5 You can then run the two halves through your thickness planer, keeping the jointer-treated surface down until the top surface is flattened. I always sight along the length of both faces of the board as I work it at the planer. If I see any evidence of undulations along its length, I re-flatten one face before I continue at the planer.

6 Here is the collection of wide boards I ripped in half, flattened and thicknessed. They are ready to be rejoined.

7 I began the jointing process at my machine jointer which established an edge exactly 90° from the face.

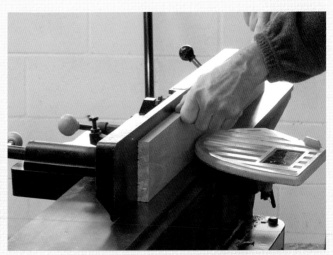

8 I then took a single shaving from those jointed edges with this low-angle, bevel-up jointer from Veritas. This tool is specifically designed to handle difficult species like curly maple. This single pass removes not only the faint ripples left behind by the machine jointer but also any tearout resulting from the curly figure, leaving behind a near-perfect surface for jointing.

9 I then clamped one board in a vise and aligned the other on edge on top of the first to verify that my edges were square.

10 I then rejoined the two halves of each board.

11 I could have surfaced the boards on my thickness planer, but I enjoy the use of planes, so I leveled each rejoined board with criss-crossing diagonal strokes of this Lie-Nielson (LN) low-angle, bevel-up jack plane, the perfect tool for flattening figured wood.

12 In this close-up, you can see the criss-crossing tracks of the jack plane. Once the surface was leveled, I removed these criss-crossing planes strokes with a smoothing plane worked in the direction of the rising grain.

13 I traced my pattern on the stock for the two end panels and bandsawed those forms.

14 I marked and cut the shelf dadoes using a stack of dado cutters on my radial arm saw. (This work could also be accomplished on the table saw.)

15 I cut the dadoes to a width slightly less than the thickness of the shelves, which gave me some thickness I could remove with a plane to fit each shelf to its dado.

16 Because I had decided to use drywall screws with their countersunk heads hidden under plugs, I next drilled the ³/₈" countersink holes using a Forstner bit.

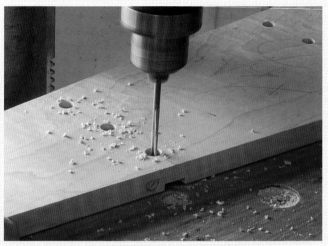

17 Then, in the center of each countersink hole, I drilled the through hole for the screws that would hold the shelf unit together. This bit is just a little larger in diameter than the threads on the drywall screws* I would be using at assembly.

* Several years ago, a reader wrote to the publisher of *Pleasant Hill Shaker Furniture* to complain about the fact that in the book I'd used drywall screws to hold the top of a Shaker table reproduction in place. He rightly felt the screws were historically inaccurate. I understand the concern, but I think it's misplaced.

First, it isn't economically possible to reproduce every historical nuance of period and Shaker originals. We're building our reproductions in the 21st century, and all of our materials and tools are results of 21st-century manufacturing processes. And these processes are written on the unseen surfaces of drawer bottoms and case sides in the form of jointer or planer ripples and the arcing tracks of circular saws. Our hardware too is marked by the consistencies of 21st-century manufacturing processes which produce, for instance, screws in which each one is the exact duplicate of the first. This is a consistency 18th-century makers of steel fasteners could not approach.

After 25 years of studying Shaker furniture and the men (and some women) who made it, I believe they would choose coarse-threaded drywall screws in many applications for the same reasons I choose them: They're inexpensive and have a holding power greater than the holding power of traditional woodscrews that have thicker shanks and narrower threads.

18 While its true the screws turned into end grain lack the holding power of screws turned into side grain, if you're careful to select a bit of the right size—one that allows the threads to bite into the sides of hole without requiring so much torque that they're twisted off—the screws still provide an acceptable amount of grip, particularly if you use several screws as I did.

As always, when installing screws, it's important to experiment with the bits you intend to use on scrap before you use those bits on the real thing.

Years ago, I cut out a number of plywood gussets like the one shown here to make it easier to glue up cabinets that were truly square. When I drilled the holes in the end grain of each shelf (for the threaded shanks of the drywall screws), I used one of these gussets to hold the shelf and the end in the proper alignment while I drilled those holes.

19 I then turned the 1¹⁄₄" coarse-threaded drywall screws into the end grain of each shelf. Notice that the shelf edges haven't yet been beveled to match the angled ends of the shelf unit.

20 I then planed the bevel on each of the top two shelves and the rounded edge on the bottom shelf.

21 After applying a bit of glue to each tapered ³⁄₈" plug, I tapped them into the countersink holes.

22 I then planed the plugs flush.

PART TWO *The Peg/Rail System*

While several of the pieces in this book are fairly accurate reproductions of original pieces, there are others, like this large shelf unit, in which I made alterations to suit my tastes and/or modern storage needs and/or modern materials. In the case of this particular unit, I probably went further afield than in the case of any other piece appearing in this book, although anyone who has seen the original in the collection of Shaker Community, Inc., in Hancock,

PROJECT FOUR

POPLAR HANGING SHELF

together, and while I think a threaded rod would supply sufficient strength, it seems an awkward solution to the joinery problem. I opted for a variation of the joinery I used to hold together the curly maple shelf unit in the previous section of this book, the only difference being the method by which I concealed the countersunk heads of the drywall screws, using buttons with domed tops here, rather than smaller buttons planed flush. You need some kind of supplemental joinery because a glued dado — like the ones appearing here and on the curly maple shelf — have very little holding power.

I also changed the thickness of the shelf ends, using material a bit over $^5/8$", instead of the $1^1/8$" stuff in the original. I thought it was too much visual weight for these components. Finally, I changed the detailing at the fronts of the shelves and the ends, substituting a set of modern-looking bevels for the rounded shapes of the originals.

If you'd like to see a photo and drawing of the original shelf unit, you can find it in John Kassay's *The Book of Shaker Furniture*.

The construction method for this shelf unit is essentially the same as it is for the previous shelf unit, so please read the material about the construction of that unit before you begin the construction of this one.

Massachusetts will immediately recognize my version as a descendant of that piece.

The original relied on its screwed wall attachments at the top and a $^1/4$" threaded rod underneath the bottom shelf to hold the unit

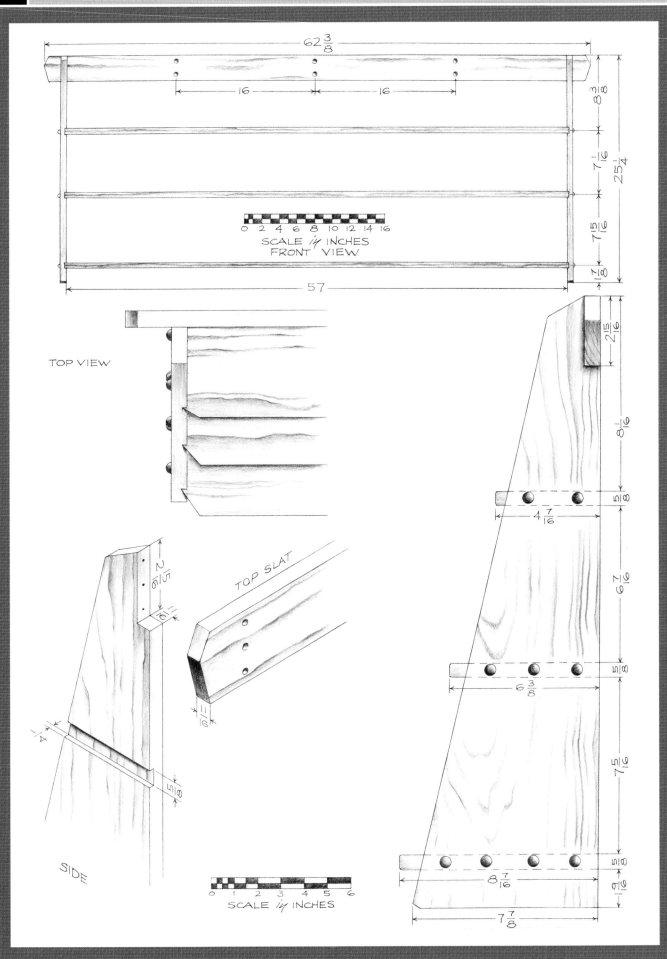

$62\frac{3}{8}$

16 16

$8\frac{3}{8}$

$7\frac{1}{16}$

$25\frac{1}{4}$

$7\frac{15}{16}$

$1\frac{7}{8}$

0 2 4 6 8 10 12 14 16

SCALE *in* INCHES
FRONT VIEW

57

TOP VIEW

$2\frac{15}{16}$

$8\frac{1}{16}$

$\frac{5}{8}$

$4\frac{7}{16}$

$6\frac{7}{16}$

$2\frac{15}{16}$

$\frac{11}{16}$

TOP SLAT

$\frac{5}{8}$

$6\frac{3}{8}$

$\frac{11}{16}$

$\frac{1}{4}$

$\frac{5}{8}$

$7\frac{5}{16}$

SIDE

0 1 2 3 4 5 6

SCALE *in* INCHES

$\frac{5}{8}$

$8\frac{7}{16}$

$1\frac{9}{16}$

$7\frac{7}{8}$

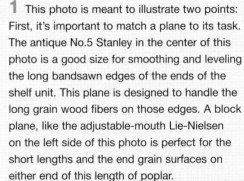

1 This photo is meant to illustrate two points: First, it's important to match a plane to its task. The antique No.5 Stanley in the center of this photo is a good size for smoothing and leveling the long bandsawn edges of the ends of the shelf unit. This plane is designed to handle the long grain wood fibers on those edges. A block plane, like the adjustable-mouth Lie-Nielsen on the left side of this photo is perfect for the short lengths and the end grain surfaces on either end of this length of poplar.

Second, you can work effectively with a plane only when it is used in the direction of rising grain. If you attempt to use it the other way, the plane will tear ugly gouges out of wood fibers and may get hung up on those fibers and refuse to cut. The direction of rising grain is indicated by the arrows I've penciled around the circumference of this shelf end.

2 After planing the top and bottom faces, and the edges smooth, I created bevels where those surfaces intersect using the Lie-Nielsen block plane.

3 At the ends of each shelf there is a small compound bevel which I marked with the shelf in its proper position in the dado.

4 Before cutting the bevel, I removed the shelf from its dado. After roughing in the bevel with a backsaw as shown here, I finished it with several strokes of a block plane.

PROJECT FIVE

KEY BOARD

Warded locks — the kind used by 19th century Americans
to secure everything from the household's sugar box to the
front door of the home — required large keys with long
shafts, simple teeth for engaging the plates in the locks, and
elaborate bows (the part you hold) on which a metal worker
often demonstrated his skill.

These keys were too large to be kept on a ring in a pocket.
While they could be carried on a ring hanging from the
waist, they were more often kept/displayed on a board used
to house all of the skeleton keys in use in a household.

This keyboard was designed to hold these large-scale skeleton keys, and although in the past when reproducing period
keyboards I've reduced their size to accommodate modern
keys, I liked the scale of this example, so I decided to build it
full size, but as usual, I tinkered with a few little details.

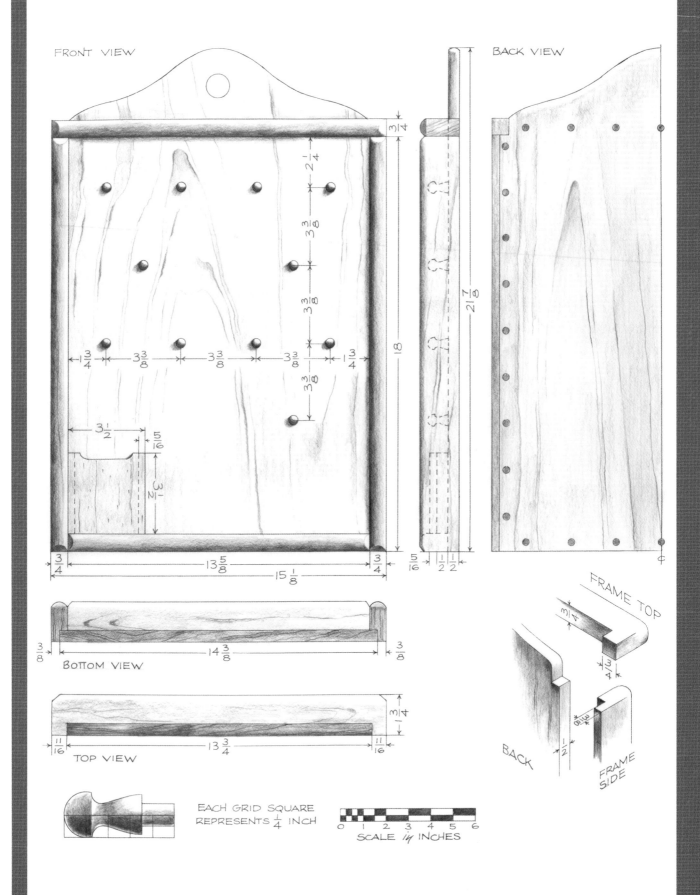

FRONT VIEW

BACK VIEW

$\frac{3}{4}$

$2\frac{1}{4}$

$3\frac{3}{8}$

$3\frac{3}{8}$

$3\frac{3}{8}$

18

$21\frac{7}{8}$

$\frac{1}{4}$ $3\frac{3}{8}$ $3\frac{3}{8}$ $3\frac{3}{8}$ $1\frac{3}{4}$

$3\frac{1}{2}$

$\frac{5}{16}$

$3\frac{1}{2}$

$\frac{3}{4}$ $13\frac{5}{8}$ $\frac{3}{4}$

$15\frac{1}{8}$

$\frac{5}{16}$ $\frac{1}{2}$ $\frac{1}{2}$

¢

FRAME TOP

$\frac{3}{4}$

$\frac{3}{4}$

$\frac{3}{16}$

BACK

$\frac{1}{2}$

FRAME SIDE

$\frac{3}{8}$ $14\frac{3}{8}$ $\frac{3}{8}$

BOTTOM VIEW

$\frac{3}{4}$

$\frac{11}{16}$ $13\frac{3}{4}$ $\frac{11}{16}$

TOP VIEW

EACH GRID SQUARE
REPRESENTS $\frac{1}{4}$ INCH

0 1 2 3 4 5 6

SCALE IN INCHES

1 In other chapters of this book, I demonstrate different methods for flattening stock prior to gluing it up, but in the case of this piece—because that material I used was generally flat to start with—I chose a simpler method. Instead of flattening the bottom of each piece before I ran it through my planer, I simply ran both the top and bottom through my planer, bringing it down almost to the desired, final thickness.

The boards were cupped before I thicknessed them, but because my planer is small, its infeed roller isn't massive enough to flatten a board before feeding it past the knives. So, the hard rubber infeed roller simply contacts the top surfaces of the cupped board and pushes the board into the cutting head, which removes the high spots. (This is one of the advantages of small machinery. The feed roller on a larger commercial grade planer will often flatten a cupped board before feeding it against the knives. The board then resumes its cupped shape when it exits the planer.)

This technique worked well in this instance for two reasons. First, the material was relatively flat to start with demonstrating only a modest amount of twist. Second, I left just enough thickness to remove that slight twist with hand planes after I'd glued up the key board's main panel.

2 This is the first of several passes to straighten one edge of this board. Because the board had a bow, I took several passes from the high, center section of that bow before addressing the whole length of the edge.

3 To check that my jointed edges were truly square, I stacked the two unglued pieces on edge in a vise. I then laid the blade of a framing square against the face of the two boards. If the jointed edges were not square, one of the boards would have leaned away from or into the square.

4 This is the arrangement I use for gluing up all panels. I position a pair of pipe clamps as shown supporting the boards I'm joining on a pair of 2x2s. These 2x2s lift the panel to the level of the pipe clamp's pressure points, which reduces the tendency of a firmly clamped panel to deform under pressure. I then clamp cleats onto the top of the panel to further ensure that the top remains in the same plane. Notice that the 2x2s and the cleats are protected from the glue with strips of newspaper.

5 I then leveled the panel to remove the slight twist using this Lie-Nielsen low-angle jack plane which is designed to handle difficult species like curly maple. I worked the surface with criss-crossing diagonal strokes until that surface was level. I repeated the process for the back face.

6 I then removed the criss-crossing jack plane strokes with this Spiers smoother, using it in the direction of the grain. I suppose I could have used a low-angle smoother on this curly-maple panel, but I love my Spiers and I haven't yet found a wood it can't tame.

7 After ripping the panel to width, I used a band saw to cut the cyma curve on the top.

8 After cutting the hang hole with a Forstner bit, I created a gentle radius for the bandsawn top using a rasp, working it between pencil lines I sketched on the edge, on the back and on the front. It is, of course, possible to create such a radius without pencil lines, but I find these make it easier to create a radius of a consistent size and shape.

9 I next rabbeted the material from which I would cut the sides. This rabbet later contained the key board back.

10 The four pieces that frame the key board have a radius on the front edges. The radius could be formed with a router or with a nosing plane. I chose to use a jack plane. First, I established three guidelines: one in the center of the edge and one each on the front and back of each piece.

11 I then roughed in the radii using multiple passes of my jack plane as shown.

12 I followed the jack plane with a rasp and sandpaper.

13 Although they weren't present on the original, I created little bevels at the ends of all four frame components. This dresses up the points where the frame components come together.

14 On my drill press, I bored the through holes for the drywall screws that would hold the back to the frame components. These holes should be just large enough to allow the screw threads to pass.

15 I then used a countersink bit to create depressions for the screw heads.

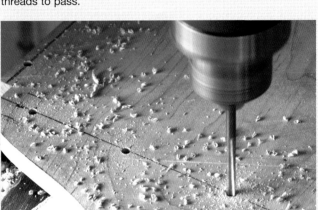

16 Before I turned in each screw, I drilled a hole for that screw in the back edge of the frame components. These holes should have a diameter a bit less than the thread diameter of the screw you're going to use. If the wood is soft like the pine in the Canterbury blanket chest which appears on page 88, this hole isn't necessary, but in a hardwood like the maple I'm working here, this hole is essential in order to avoid snapping off screws as you turn them in. (As always, it's best to test bit sizes by turning screws into blocks of scrap.)

17 I turned in each of the screws.

18 I then laid out and drilled the holes for the tenons on the backs of each of the tiny Shaker pegs from which the keys would hang. I used craft-shop pegs because I don't have the tiny turning tools such pegs require. (The pegs I used were manufactured by a company called Wood Shoppe and were priced at $1.47 per dozen. I found mine in a local Hobby Lobby.)

19 I put a spot of glue on each tenon and tapped it into place with a mallet.

20 I glued and clamped the three components for the key pocket.

21 After that glue had dried, I brushed a little glue on the back edges (and the outside face of the compartment) and pressed it into place. If you hold an assembly like this in place for 60 seconds, the glue will grab and create a joint that's just as strong as if it had been clamped.

PROJECT ONE

OVAL BOXES

While the Shakers are rightly known for all manner of storage furniture and woodenware, the two storage concepts with which they are most closely associated are the peg rail system and the oval box system, with the oval box system being paramount in the public consciousness. For many, when they think Shaker, the think of the delightfully elegant bentwood boxes, churned out by the thousands in some Shaker communities.

Of course, the bentwood box wasn't invented by American Shakers. The idea predates the founding of the Shaker experiment in communal living by many centuries, but the Shakers gave the concept its definitive forms, adding gracefully contoured fingers and a distinctive oval shape.

There's more than one way to make an oval box, and I have described several different methods on the pages of books and magazines over the last 20 years, and I think each one I describe is better than the last, but all will work, and so too will the many methods developed by other craftsmen.

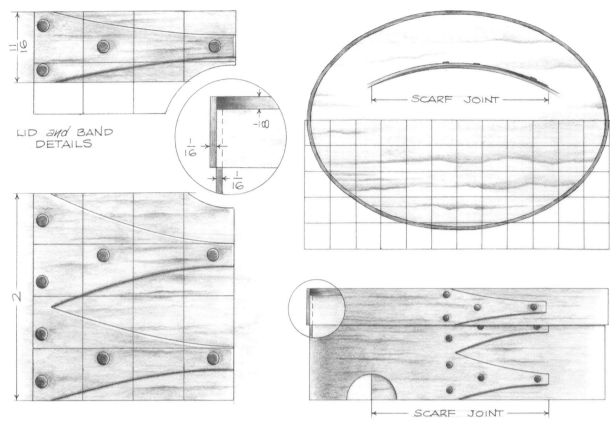

LID *and* BAND
DETAILS

SCARF JOINT

SCALE *in* INCHES
DETAILS

EACH GRID SQUARE
REPRESENTS ½ INCH

SCALE *in* INCHES

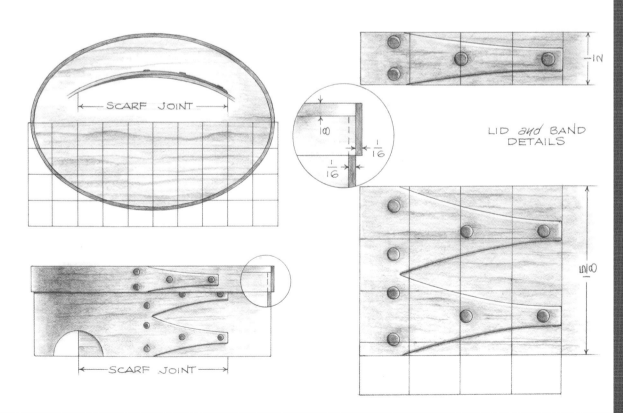

SCARF JOINT

LID *and* BAND
DETAILS

SCARF JOINT

1 During a trip to Pleasant Hill, Kentucky, in December of 2007 to measure pieces for this book, I set up a shot of a stack of oval boxes in front of a window in a room on the second floor of the Meeting House, and I noticed a group of visitors huddled from the rain in the doorway of the Centre Family Dwelling across the gravel turnpike. I took this shot, which proves that—at least for me—it's better to be lucky than good.

2 While most contemporary oval boxes are sold with a natural finish, many of the 19th-century boxes made by the hands of Shaker craftsmen were painted, as these sponge-painted examples from Pleasant Hill demonstrate. While makers of contemporary boxes are nearly invariable in aligning the end of the lid finger with the ends of the box fingers, a fair percentage of original Shaker boxes fail to demonstrate this consistent alignment, as you can see on the top and bottom boxes in this stack.

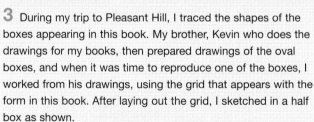

3 During my trip to Pleasant Hill, I traced the shapes of the boxes appearing in this book. My brother, Kevin who does the drawings for my books, then prepared drawings of the oval boxes, and when it was time to reproduce one of the boxes, I worked from his drawings, using the grid that appears with the form in this book. After laying out the grid, I sketched in a half box as shown.

4 Then, after folding the paper, I went to a window and traced my half box. When the paper was opened up, I then had both halves of a perfectly symmetrical box.

5 A box begins with a mould which should be exactly the same size as the interior of the finished box. Here, I'm sanding the sides of a bandsawn maple mould.

7 I used a metal cutting blade in my saber saw like the one I'm holding in my hand. Notice also that I kept that blade well outside of the scratched lines on the saw blade.

6 Unlike many boxmakers who peen their tacks on an anvil—often a length of metal pipe—I peen the tacks on my boxes on bits of sheet steel I've inlaid into my moulds. I cut the sheet steel for this mould from a handsaw I picked up at an antique mall for $2.

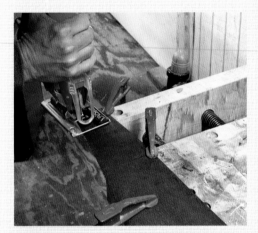

8 I then worked my way up to the lines on my grinder.

9 I cut a shallow mortise for the sheet steel in my mould. This sheet of steel was positioned so that it would be underneath all the copper tacks I would later peen to hold the box bands together. The first column of tacks—the one just to the left of the fingers on the completed box—should be halfway across the length of one side of the finished box with the other two columns of tacks to the right of that, so I positioned the sheet metal accordingly.

10 I then attached the metal plate to the mould with contact cement.

11 I began preparing box band material by squaring up a piece of hard maple on the jointer.

12 I've tried several different fences on my band saw, and while they all more or less work, stock inevitably seems to wander, no matter how careful I am about establishing the blade's angle of drift. I prefer sawing to a line, so the next step was marking the 1/8" thickness of the unplaned band stock.

13 I then sawed a leaf of band stock from the maple square. (If you're working on a relatively small band saw like mine, there's an upper limit on the width of band stock you can prepare. I've found that—even with a sharp blade and a slow feed rate—it's hard for me to resaw hardwood stock that's more than 5" wide.)

14 I applied double-sided tape to a length of pine wide enough and long enough to back up the leaves of band stock.

15 I then taped a leaf of band stock to the pine with the sawn face up. I used several passes to remove the band saw marks. The bit of band material in my left hand is my gauge to tell me when I've reached the desired thickness.

16 With a chisel, I levered the band stock from the pine.

17 I rip box and lid bands to width using a utility knife. Notice the finger patterns to the right of my left hand.

18 After tracing the finger patterns on the band stock, I roughed in the fingers on the band saw using a fine-toothed blade.

19 I cut the bevels on each finger using a utility knife.

20 The bevels on the tips of the fingers are best cut with a chisel.

21 The unfingered ends of box and lid bands need to be feathered down to nothing. Most box makers create this taper in thickness on a sander. I prefer to use a smoothing plane.

22 I mark and pre-drill all the tack holes before soaking the bands.

23 Oval box-maker John Wilson is, I think, the only source for copper, box-making tacks seen here in the two envelopes. These tacks come in several sizes and if you tell John (517-543-5325) the thickness of the box bands you'll be joining, he can tell you which size you'll need.

24 It's necessary to plasticize box bands in water before bending them around the box forms. Hot water plasticizes better than cold water, but I have bent bands after soaking them in cold water. I bring water to a boil in the deep-fat fryer on the right, then pour the boiling water into the plastic tub on the left. Bands should be ready to bend after a thirty-minute soak.

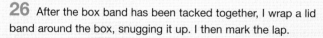

26 After the box band has been tacked together, I wrap a lid band around the box, snugging it up. I then mark the lap.

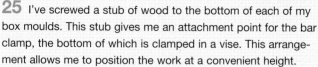

25 I've screwed a stub of wood to the bottom of each of my box moulds. This stub gives me an attachment point for the bar clamp, the bottom of which is clamped in a vise. This arrangement allows me to position the work at a convenient height.

A split can run around a band between the band's fingers if you lose your grip on one of the fingers during the process of wrapping the band around a box mould. I use a flexible caul made of thin strips of wood fastened together with duct tape as shown here. This caul allows me to easily hold all the fingers down until I can get some tacks in them to prevent splitting.

People who haven't made oval boxes often think the fingers are glued to the band, but the truth is that the box bands are held together with nothing but the peened tips of the tiny copper tacks, the heads of which you see on the outside of the box. The shanks of the tacks are slightly longer than the thickness of the double lap of band material. When the tacks are driven through the thickness of the fingers and the band, the tips of the tacks strike the metal (cemented on the box mould) and mushroom, creating a joint of surprising strength.

Many boxmakers use wooden forms to wrap their bands, then move the wrapped box bands to an anvil to peen the tacks. This eliminates the need for the inlaid sheet steel I use on my box moulds.

27 I drive tacks into the lid band, peening them on a pipe that I use as an anvil.

28 I used figured material for the lids on these boxes, and figured material is notorious for tearing out when it's run through a planer. A card scraper can quickly smooth torn-out areas.

30 Before marking the lid material, I taped the lid band to the box band, taking care to align the box and lid fingers. I then upended the taped bands onto the lid material and marked around the inside of the lid band. Again, it's important to press the bands onto the material so that there is no deformation.

29 I pressed the tacked and dried box band against the material from which I would cut the bottom, then drew around the inside of the band on that material. It's important to press the band carefully against the bottom material so that the tacked band isn't deformed as the bottom is being marked.

Preparation of material for lids and bottoms is one of the trickiest parts of oval box making because even the tiniest bit of shrinkage across the grain will leave a lid or bottom looking sloppy in its band, and it's tough to get solid material dry enough to completely eliminate this shrinkage.

Many years ago I did a book for another publisher on the subject of Shaker woodenware. I made a half dozen oval boxes for that book, then shipped the boxes—as well as many other pieces—to New York to be photographed for the book. When the boxes left my shop, the quarter-sawn white pine lids and bottoms were tight in their bands. After the materials got to New York, they were stored for several months in a hot, dry warehouse. By the time the photographer was ready to shoot them, a good bit of shrinkage had occurred, leaving the lid and bottom stock looking very sloppy in their bands.

I was horrified by images the publisher sent me.

Fortunately, the publisher had just started using software to manipulate images and they were able to close up those gaps in the photos, so the boxes looked good in the book, but the message for me was clear: Spare no effort in preparing material for lids and bottoms.

The best material for such an application is plywood, because it doesn't shrink as it dries, but plywood isn't traditional, so today when I'm planning a run of oval boxes, I'll start prepping lid and bottom stock months in advance, stickering it in a dry, airy corner of the house. During those months, I'll flatten and thickness the material at various times, letting it season between these wood-prepping sessions.

31 I cut out the lid and bottom discs, keeping the blade of my band saw well outside the penciled lines.

32 I set the table on my disc sander to a 5° angle. This allows me to tightly fit the discs inside the bands.

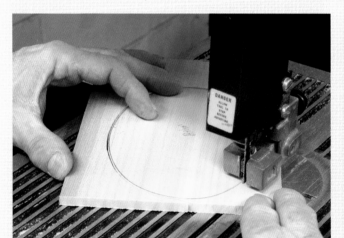

33 When sanding lid discs, the top of the disc should be up. When sanding bottom discs, the bottom of the disc should be up. This permits the 5° angle of the table to give you a little assist when sliding bands over discs. This disc-sanding process requires a little artistry. The object is to get the lid to fit the inside of the band perfectly at exactly the same moment the disc is sanded to a perfect oval. It rarely works out to perfection, but that is the goal toward which I work each time I fit the discs to the bands.

34 The easiest way to fit a tight disc into a box band is to place the disc on the bench and then slip the band over it. Remember to align the band so that the first row of tacks is at the midline of the box's horizontal width.

35 Before slipping the lid band around the lid disc, I place the disc on the box and mark the end of the box fingers on the lid disc. This tells me where to align the end of the lid-band fingers.

36 The box and lid bands can be attached to their discs with either wood pegs (typically cut from toothpicks) or brads. I usually use brads because I think they're easier to install successfully. Both fasteners require that you pre-drill insertion holes. In this photo, you can see that the bit I use for pre-drilling brad insertion holes is very nearly the same diameter as the brad.

37 On a small box like this, I use four brads each in the lid and box disc. Larger boxes require more fasteners.

38 I drive the brads into place with a tack hammer.

This is the original sponge-painted Pleasant Hill box that I'm reproducing.

PROJECT ONE

EIGHT-DRAWER JEWELRY CASE: A SEWING CHEST CONVERSION

In addition to the construction of many imaginative built-in storage units, Shaker craftsmen excelled in the design and construction of free-standing pieces. Some of these were quite small, like the small chest appearing on page 126. Others are much larger, like the Hamlin cupboard from Pleasant Hill which appears on page 132. (These pieces may need to be reduced in size to fit into today's American homes.)

The original chest of drawers on which this project is based was likely made in Canterbury, New Hampshire (a Shaker community in the middle of the 19th century) to be used as auxiliary storage next to a sewing desk. The top drawer of the original was fitted with ranks of upright dowels to hold spools of thread. My version of that original is fitted with dowels in the top drawer as well, but in my version those dowels are intended to hold rings, rather than spools of thread because my version of this chest is meant to be used as large jewelry case, rather than as storage for sewing accessories.

The drawers of the Canterbury original are nailed together, but I decided to use a different method of drawer construction, one I'd been considering for some time. I decided to assemble my drawers using dowel joints. To streamline the joint-making process, I designed a very simple jig, and the results were even better than I'd hoped.

Since the piece was being redesigned to hold jewelry, I ordered a flocking kit (from Woodcraft) to line the ring drawer, as well as several trays I was adding to the second and third drawers to hold necklaces, bracelets and earrings.

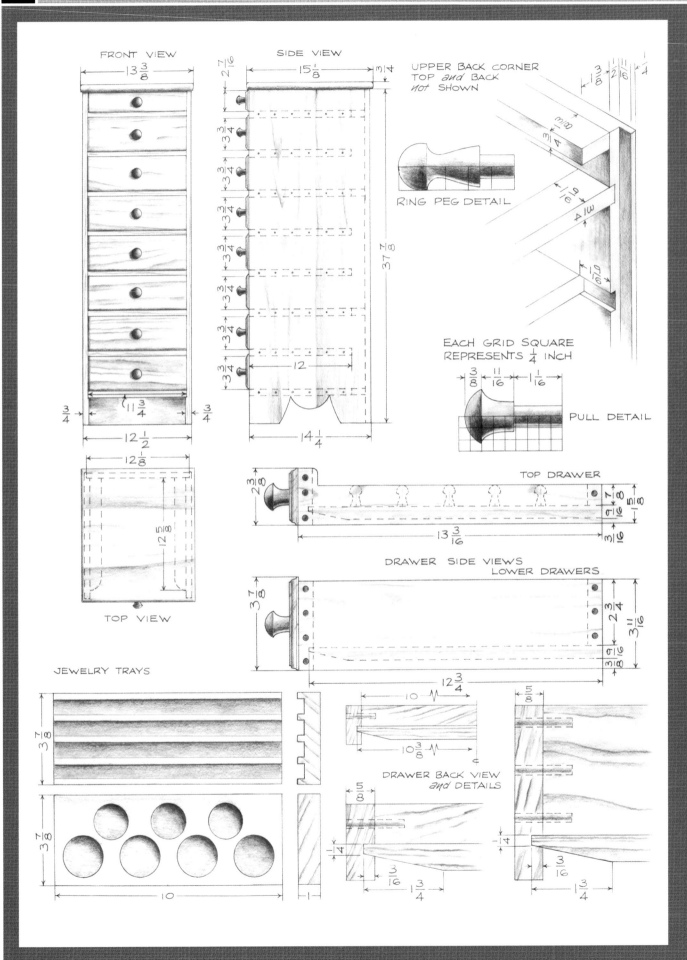

FRONT VIEW

SIDE VIEW

UPPER BACK CORNER
TOP *and* BACK
not SHOWN

RING PEG DETAIL

EACH GRID SQUARE
REPRESENTS $\frac{1}{4}$ INCH

PULL DETAIL

TOP VIEW

TOP DRAWER

DRAWER SIDE VIEWS
LOWER DRAWERS

JEWELRY TRAYS

DRAWER BACK VIEW
and DETAILS

1 To simplify construction, I decided to use full dust panels instead of drawer runners. Because my primary wood was poplar—which I was finishing natural—and because poplar is more expensive than the No.2 white pine I used as a secondary wood, I glued up the dust panel stock with poplar on the front and white pine on the back. In this photo, you can see some of the dust-panel stock prior to glue up.

2 I edge-jointed the stock on my jointer.

3 I then took a single shaving with a jointing plane to remove the slight ripples the machine jointer left behind. I paid only $30 for this 28" antique Ohio Tool jointing plane. It has a nearly unused iron (the iron and cap iron alone are worth $100). I flattened the sole, grafted in a little bit of scrap to tighten the mouth and ended up with a first-class jointing plane, which is the functional equal of new jointing planes costing hundreds of dollars. Although I like my metal jointing planes, they are quite heavy, and this wooden equivalent makes sense if you're going to spend much time flattening large panels.

4 I glued up the various panels this jewelry case required using the method you see here. The 2x2s under the panel raised the panel to the center pressure of the pipe clamps. I clamped cleats on either end of the panel to ensure that the panel remained flat under the pressure of the pipe clamps. Both the 2x2s and the cleats were protected from the glue by strips of newspaper. In this photo, I'm making a flatness check with the blade of a framing square.

5 Because the panels were too wide for both my machine jointer and my thickness planer, I leveled them with criss-crossing diagonal strokes of a jack plane, followed by lengthwise strokes of a jointing plane.

6 I then smoothed the surface of the exterior panels with a smoothing plane. Those panels which would be used as dust panels between drawers didn't require anything more than the criss-crossing jack-plane work.

7 After ripping the sides to width and cross-cutting them to length, I traced the arches' pattern on the bottoms of the sides and cut the arches on my band saw.

8 I then cut a rabbet on the inside back edge of the two side panels using a set of dado cutters on my table saw. I clamped a length of scrap to the metal fence of my table saw so I could work next to that fence without damaging either the dado cutters or the metal fence.

9 With a stack of dado cutters on my radial arm saw, I cut the dadoes on the interior surfaces of the chest sides for the many dust panels this chest of drawers requires.

10 The top has a radius all around which I formed with multiple passes of a Lie-Nielsen low-angle jack plane. The first step in creating such a radius in this manner is the placement of three pencil lines on each edge. One line marks the center of the edge. The other two are placed on the top and bottom surfaces of the panel. The placement of these last two lines is determined by the steepness of the desired radius. The farther the lines are placed from the edge, the more extreme the radius.

11 In order to later fasten the top to the sides of the chest, I had to first attach cleats to the sides using 1 5/8" coarse-threaded drywall screws. Before I installed the screws, I drilled countersink holes in the cleats deep enough to give me significant penetration into the case sides without coming through the sides. Here I'm checking the depth of the countersunk holes.

12 I then attached the cleats. Notice they are already drilled for the screws that will pass through them into the bottom surface of the case top.

13 Once I had screwed the lid onto the top of the two sides, I began fitting dust panels into their dadoes. I left the dust panel stock thick so that a bit of excess thickness could be planed away at assembly. This ensured a tight fit in the dadoes.

14 I prefer the organized look of carefully spaced nails to the disorganized look of nails spaced by the eye. This marking aide allowed me to achieve consistent spacing of the nails that passed through the sides of the case into the dust panels.

15 Typically, a home-improvement store will stock several different kinds of small-headed nails which are often informally grouped under the term "finish" or "finishing" nails. These nails have small heads with a slight dimple in the top center. This provides a registration point for the tip of a nail set used to punch the head of the nail below the surface of the wood. The small depression left by the setting of the nail is usually filled with putty or colored wax.

Some of these finishing nails are zinc coated, which makes them too thick for most indoor applications. Most, however, are bright, uncoated nails. Finishing nails look like casing nails which are used to install interior woodwork (like the door casing for which they are named. These are relatively thick in cross section with a great deal of strength.) Finish nails, on the other hand, are thinner in cross section and are noticeably less resistant to stresses than casing nails. However, for some finish-work applications, finish nails are preferred because they are less likely to split the stock in which they are driven, and they leave a smaller hole to fill.

I chose to fasten the dust panels to the sides of the case using a large number of finishing nails with the heads set and the holes filled.

In this photo, I'm driving the 7d finish nails I chose for this application. Poplar is a relatively soft hardwood. I could, therefore, drive these thin-shanked nails without first pre-drilling.

16 I then followed up with a nail set, punching the head of each nail about $1/16$" below the surface of the wood.

17 I set each dust panel so that the front edge stood slightly proud of the front edges of the case sides in order to leave me with material to plane flush.

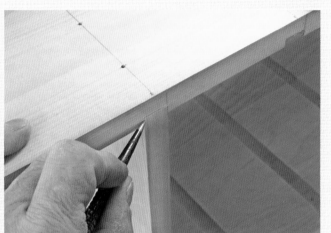

18 With a block plane, I leveled these edges.

19 With a stack of dado cutters on my table saw, I cut rabbets on the ends of the back side of the drawer fronts to create a lip for each drawer.

20 I then cut a rabbet on the top of the drawer as well.

21 Dado cutters leave behind a fairly rough surface. I cleaned these up with shoulder planes. The drawer front on the left is straight from the dado cutters, while the drawer front on the right has been treated with shoulder planes.

22 The only significant change I made in the exterior appearance of my chest of drawers is the profile around the drawers. Instead of the simple radius of the Shaker original, I created a more detailed lip using a $5/32$" Roman ogee router bit because I thought the drawers benefited from the extra shadow lines.

23 I first cut the profile on the two ends, then on the long sides of each drawer front.

24 Using dado cutters on my table saw, I cut the grooves for the drawer bottoms on the back sides of the drawer fronts and on the insides of the drawer sides.

25 This simple jig allowed me to hold parts in the correct alignment while drilling the holes for the dowels I used to join the drawer parts. (The triangle screwed to the upright was included simply to keep the upright component square.)

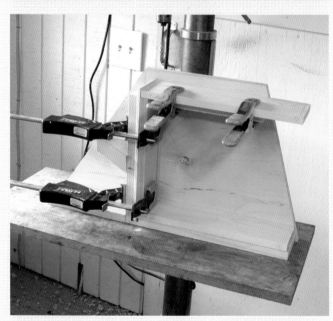

26 I clamped the drawer front (or back) to the upright on the left side of the jig and the drawer side to the horizontal shelf of the jig. Aligning the two parts in the same configuration as the finished drawer, with the ends of the drawer sides lapping the rabbet of the drawer front (or the full width of the end on the drawer back).

27 I moved the jig so the drill bit was aligned with the marks I'd made on the drawer side to locate the dowels. I then brought the bit down into the work to a depth of about $1^1/_2$".

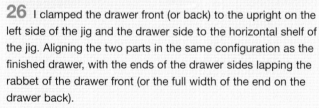

28 I glued up short lengths of dowel and tapped them into the holes, passing through the drawer sides and into the end grain of the drawer front and drawer back.

29 I then sawed off the surplus length of the dowels.

30 Before I set the drawer aside to cure, I checked to see that the sides were correctly aligned and square.

31 Next, I bored the mortises for the drawer pulls. I clamped a caul to the back of the drawer front to keep the drill bit from breaking out chips on the inside of the drawer front.

32 I planed off the dowels stubs. The stubs on the back of the drawer can be planed with a block plane, but to work up close to the lip on the drawer front, you must have either a shoulder plane (shown at right) or a rabbet plane.

33 When using a shoulder plane in this context, you must take care to keep the sole parallel to the work in order to avoid having the side of the plane's iron dig into the work.

34 Before I installed the drawer bottoms, I evened out any irregularities in the top and bottom edges of the drawer frame's parts.

35 I created raised panels for the drawer bottoms using a fore plane as shown here. I started by marking two lines on each drawer bottom. One indicated the final desired thickness on the three edges of the bottom that would be beveled. The other indicated the width of that bevel. I simply planed a bevel connecting those two lines.

36 At the back of each drawer bottom, I cut a notch, just wide enough for the shank of a screw. Then, after sliding the drawer bottom into its grooves on the inside of the drawer sides, I turned a screw up into the bottom edge of the drawer back.

37 Each knob requires the creation of three shape elements: The dome on the top of the pull, the cove below the dome and the tenon. I fashioned the cove with a fingernail gouge by standing the tool on its side with the flute facing the cove I would create, then rolling the gouge onto its back as I simultaneously moved it into the cove. This scooping action—with the bevel riding securely on the cove—produces a cove with very little tearout.

38 I created the dome at the top of the knob with a $1/2$" skew by first creating space for the tool with repeated passes of the skew, then finishing with several paring cuts in which the tip of the skew pushed a thin roll of material across the surface of the dome. This paring cut leaves behind a surface requiring little, if any, sanding.

39 After roughing in the tenon with a fingernail gouge, I finalized the tenon with a wide, sharp chisel laid bevel side down on my tool rest as shown.

40 It's possible to turn a whole string of pulls from the same length of walnut, but it can get a little whippy in the middle unless it's supported by a steady rest. My steady rest is the palm of my off hand.

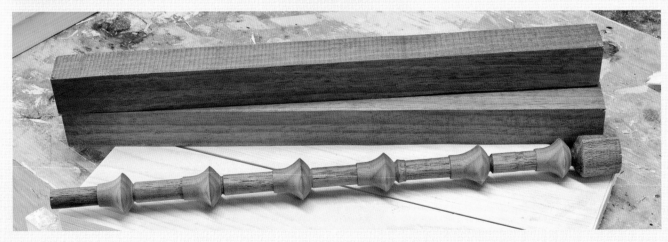

41 After sawing the pulls apart on the band saw, I finished the dome of each with a little rasp work and some sandpaper.

42 After gluing the knob tenons into their mortises, I began to fit each drawer to its opening. This process requires a little detective work because it's not always obvious why a drawer refuses to slide smoothly. It's necessary to study all the contact surfaces throughout the drawer's full range of motion, then remove material from problem areas with a plane, one shaving at a time.

43 I made the necklace and bracelet trays with repeated passes over a stack of dado cutters.

44 The earring compartments were created with two different sizes of Forstner bits.

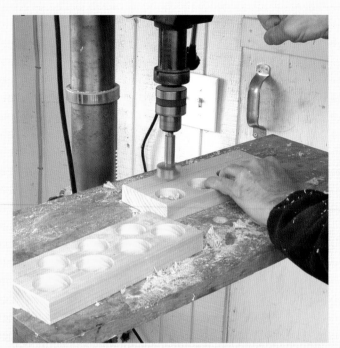

45 I don't think I've ever used pre-fabricated parts—that is until I built this jewelry case. I wanted some tiny Shaker pegs to use as mooring points for rings in the ring drawer, and I found exactly what I needed at a local Hobby Lobby at a reasonable price. When you compare the pegs to my turning tools, I think you can appreciate why I'm not equipped to turn my own mini pegs. The pegs I used were manufactured by a company called Wood Shoppe and were priced at $1.47 per dozen.

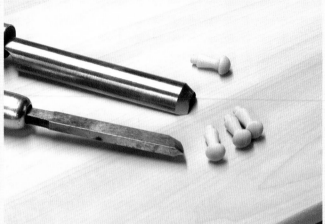

46 I coated the interior surfaces of the earring and necklace/bracelet trays, as well as the interior surfaces of the ring drawer with wine-colored DonJer flocking purchased from Woodcraft. (Wine flocking: 17C23, wine undercoat adhesive: 17H42, mini flocker: 127115.)

47 Before applying the undercoat adhesive, I sealed the surfaces of the trays and drawer. Then, after masking the surfaces that would be left unflocked, I coated the surfaces that would receive flocking with a fairly heavy coat of wine-colored undercoat adhesive. The adhesive shouldn't be applied so heavily that it puddles, but it must not be brushed out to a transparent thinness because it won't provide enough holding power for the flocking. Then, after filling the flocker about halfway full of loose flocking, I pumped the flocker between my hands while simultaneously rotating it to keep the flocking inside in a state of agitation. The flocking is then dispersed through the openings

on one end of the flocker onto the surfaces being worked. I applied the material quite heavily and then—after several days of drying—I upended the parts, which caused the surplus flocking (it can be reused) to fall from those parts.

48 I then drilled holes for the two rows of mini Shaker pegs that would serve as ring posts.

49 I installed the pegs with a drop of glue on each tenon.

50 With a sanding block and paper, I cleaned up the edges where the unflocked and flocked surfaces meet.

51 This project, like every other unpainted project in this book, was finished with several coats of Minwax wipe-on polyurethane. After prepping the surfaces with a thorough sanding using 150-, 220-, 320- and 400-grit sandpapers.

PROJECT TWO

CANTERBURY BLANKET CHEST

The original of this blanket chest was built in the Canterbury, New Hampshire, Shaker community and is housed in the collection of the Greenfield Village and Henry Ford Museum in Dearborn, Michigan. I was not able to measure this piece, so I scaled up a drawing based on a photo in John Kassay's *The Book of Shaker Furniture*.

I changed the moulded shapes around the lid and on the top edge of the plinth components to suit moulding planes in my collection. Choose moulding shapes for which you have profiling tools, whether those tools are moulding planes, shaper cutters or router bits.

The original was painted yellow, and since I already had one yellow box in this book I decided to paint the chest red and leave the plinth and lid moulding natural.

Locks for Solid Wood Chests

The lock I used on this chest has a fixed post rising from the plate mounted on the underside of the lid. That post is designed to fit into the case of the lock mechanism. The lock works beautifully now, but it won't work after a few years in a home with forced-air heat. The solid wood lid will shrink across its width and the post will no longer align with the lock mechanism in the front of the chest.

I've installed dozens of similar locks and the result is always the same. Orion Henderson of Horton Brasses understands, observing that "Every old chest or box I have seen has had the receiver from the lock removed, I assume for this reason." When I asked if his company would manufacture a lock with an adjustable post that could be repositioned as the lid shrank, he said: "The principle of an adjustable lock is good but economics stands in the way of implementation. The demand for these types of locks is limited and tooling changes would be cost prohibitive."

Here's how I've handled the problem: Over time, when the lock no longer closes, I remove the plate the post is attached to, plug the screw holes and reposition the plate.

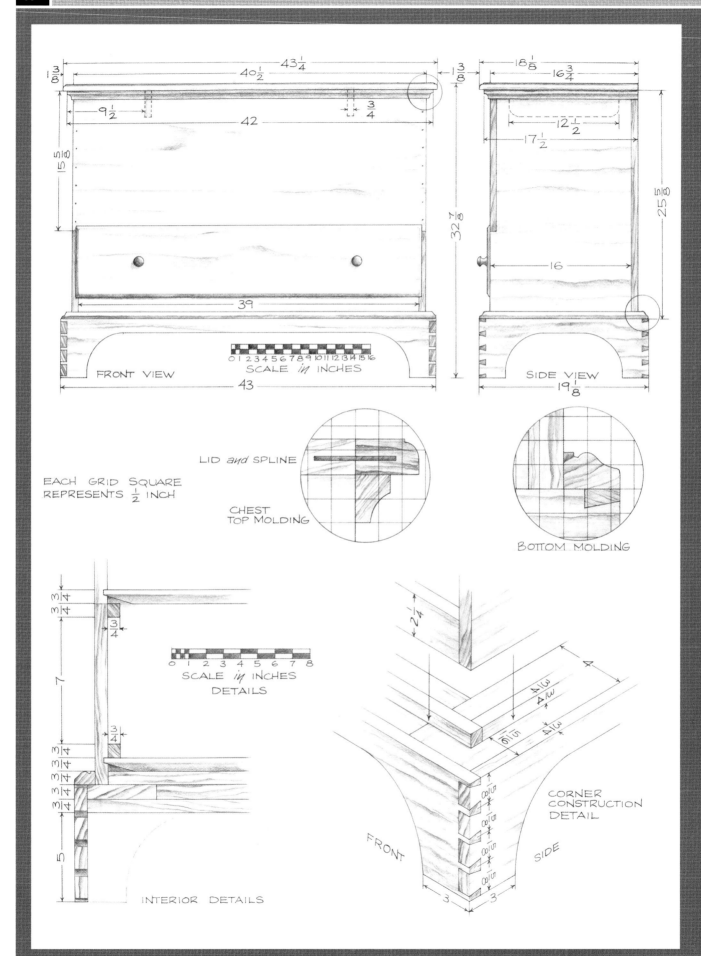

FRONT VIEW

SCALE *in* INCHES

SIDE VIEW

EACH GRID SQUARE
REPRESENTS $\frac{1}{2}$ INCH

LID *and* SPLINE

CHEST
TOP MOLDING

BOTTOM MOLDING

SCALE *in* INCHES
DETAILS

INTERIOR DETAILS

CORNER
CONSTRUCTION
DETAIL

FRONT

SIDE

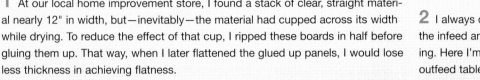

1 At our local home improvement store, I found a stack of clear, straight material nearly 12" in width, but—inevitably—the material had cupped across its width while drying. To reduce the effect of that cup, I ripped these boards in half before gluing them up. That way, when I later flattened the glued up panels, I would lose less thickness in achieving flatness.

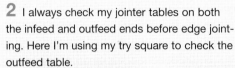

2 I always check my jointer tables on both the infeed and outfeed ends before edge jointing. Here I'm using my try square to check the outfeed table.

3 I then arrange the narrow boards into the wide panels the project will require, marking them with a pencil scribble as shown here, so I'll remember to assemble them in this same way during glue up. It's important that the narrow boards arranged at this stage in the process are longer than the final panel needs to be and will yield more width than the final panel needs. It's also important—even on a project like this one that will be covered in paint—to think about an "A" and "B" side.

4 I then edge-joint all of the mating edges the panel requires. (I also follow up the machine jointer with one pass using a good jointing plane. This final pass removes any ripples the jointer might have left on this joint. I do this despite the fact that years of experience have told me that it's possible to go straight from the jointer to glue up—as long as the final pass on the jointer is done slowly, taking a relatively thin cut.)

5 Once the narrow boards have been edge jointed, I check to make sure all my joints are properly formed. To make this check, I stack the boards on edge, holding the bottom board in a vise. I then align a straight edge with the front face of the stack to verify that the front face of all the boards lies in the same plane. I finish the check by lowering my head and scanning the joints between boards. If there are any light gaps visible (or if the face isn't in the same plane), I re-joint the edges.

6 After a dry run with all my clamps and cauls, I spread glue on the surfaces to be mated.

8 This close up shows the amount of glue squeezeout you should expect from a well-clamped edge joint.

7 This is the method I use for clamping wide panels. I place clamps on alternating faces of the panel, spacing them about 10"-15" apart, depending on the length of the panel. I support the panel on two cleats, which raise the panel to the height of the clamp heads' pressure points. If I lay the panel directly on the pipes, the clamp heads' pressure points would be above the thickness of the panel with the result that the panel might buckle when I tighten the clamp heads. I also add cauls to the top surface of the panel, clamping them to the panel as shown. Without these cauls, panels have a tendency to distort under the pressure of the clamps. Notice that both the cleats on the under side of the panel and the cauls on the upper side are protected from the glue with strips of newspaper.

9 If you have a 24" jointer and a 24" thickness planer, you could turn to those tools at this point, but my guess is that most craftsmen who read this are like me and lack such high powered tooling.

That's why the versatility of hand planes is so important. With a few relatively inexpensive* hand planes, you can do the same work as those mighty machines—and have fun doing it.

When I'm leveling a large glued up panel like this, I start with a plane in the fore (Stanley No.6) or jack (Stanley No.5) size. In this photo, I'm using an antique Stanley No.6 I bought for next to nothing and reconditioned.

I do the preliminary leveling by taking diagonal passes across the panel with the plane set to remove a fairly thick shaving. If your plane is well setup and properly sharp, you can level one side of pine panel this size in about 10 minutes.

(* The planes are "inexpensive" if you buy antiques and restore them. If you buy new, top-quality planes of the three sizes I'm using here—fore, jointing, and smoothing—that can run into some significant money, but even new high-quality planes—like those made by Lie-Nielsen and Veritas—come to only a fraction of the cost of a jointer and thickness planer large enough to handle panels this wide.).

10 As you can see after a few passes with my No.6, all the irregularities at the joints and all the cupping have been removed. Notice that the plane tracks cross each other because I worked the diagonals in two different directions.

11 I follow the No.6 with a jointing plane (a tool over 20" in length, like the antique Stanley No.7 I'm using here) run in the direction of rising grain. The fore plane removes gross irregularities, while the jointing plane—set to take a thinner shaving—levels the tracks left by the fore plane.

12 When you're planing a board lengthwise, working the plane in the direction of rising grain is likely to result in very smooth surfaces, while working against the direction of rising grain will likely result in a surface that shows where wood fibers have been torn out.

You can often determine the direction of rising grain by running your hand lengthwise along the surface of the board. In one direction the board feels smooth. That's the direction of rising grain and the direction you'll want to plane. Sliding your hand along the board in the opposite direction, you'll notice that surface feels a little rougher. That's the direction in which you do not want to plane.

Sometimes you can make a decision about the direction of the rising grain by looking at the edge of the board, but the very best way when you're unsure is to take a shaving with a smoothing plane over a questionable area. This is what I've done in this area. By examining the little depressions left by torn-out wood fibers, you can determine the proper direction in which to work your jointer.

14 When you're working with good planes, the surface your last smoother leaves behind is incredibly smooth, waxen, even faintly reflective. This is a surface you simply can't achieve with sandpaper (which roughens that surface by scratching it with abrasives).

13 Final surfacing is done with smoothing planes. I'm lucky enough to have a number of top-quality smoothers, like the two infills I'm using here, but a restored Stanley No.3 or No.4 will also do this work. I have my smoothers set to take shavings of several different thicknesses. The coarsest—most rank—plane takes a thinner shaving than either the fore plane or the jointer. My other smoothers take progressively thinner shavings, ending with one plane that takes a shaving so thin it doesn't quite hold together.

When you're working with a material that planes as nicely as pine, you can often produce a final surface with a good smoother, a surface that requires little or no attention with sandpaper.

15 After ripping the panels to width and cross-cutting them to length, I plowed the grooves using a stack of dado cutters on my table saw. These grooves will accept the bottom of the case. I also plowed the grooves for the bottom of the case's upper compartment at this time.

16 I create raised panels for drawer and chest bottoms with jack or fore planes. I start by laying out two pencil lines: one on the edge of the panel, indicating the desired final thickness at that edge and the other on the bottom surface of the panel 1-1 $\frac{1}{2}$" from the edge. I then use the plane to create a bevel connecting the two lines as shown here.

17 My fore plane is set to take a thick shaving because on these raised panels a little grain tearout isn't a problem.

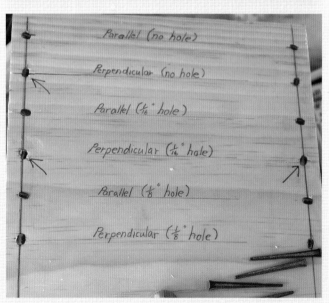

18 Like the Shaker original I was reproducing, I decided to nail the chest's upper case together. I ordered a bag of cut nails ($1\frac{3}{4}$", N-19 in the Horton Brasses catalog) like those likely used on the original from Horton Brasses. Before I started using the nails, I did some experimenting to see how they might be used to best effect.

As you can see in this photo, the best result is achieved when using them with a $\frac{1}{8}$" through hole in the top board, aligning the nail so its thickness, not its width, follows the direction of the grain. (Sometimes the nails rotated slightly as they were being driven.)

19 Before I did any nailing, I laid out pencil lines indicating the center of the thickness I would be nailing into.

20 After nailing the back panel to one end, I had an "oops" moment in which I realized I'd forgotten to install the cleats that would act as runners and kicker strips for the drawer. In this photo, I'm belatedly installing those cleats.

21 After 40 years in the shop, I've developed some work habits that make jobs like this much simpler than they were early in my career. I've learned that you simply can't do good work if the parts you're working with aren't secured, and because I work alone, securing parts sometimes means cobbling up some goofy looking constructions like the one you see here. To hold the end panels upright, I've clamped one to the side of a footstool, which is itself clamped to my bench, and I've clamped the other end panel to the little box I made for testing cut nails.

22 I'm nailing the last component in place—a filler strip that will sit just beneath the drawer front. Note that the case was assembled around the raised-panel bottoms of the case and the case's upper compartment.

23 Because I plowed through-grooves for the two raised-panel bottoms, I needed to install plugs where those grooves showed on the ends of the case. At the top left, you'll see an unplugged groove. I'm sawing off a tapered plug I glued into another groove end.

24 After the case was assembled and all the groove ends plugged, using a low-angle jack plane, I planed the end grain on the front and back panels flush with the end panels.

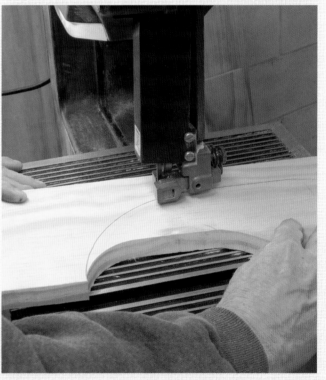

25 Rather than make patterns for the front and ends of the plinth, I made a single pattern for the curved sections of these components and used it where necessary.

26 I then cut out the curved parts on the band saw.

27 Most of the band saw marks can be removed with a block plane, but those on the curves and the flats approaching the curves must be cleaned up with other tools: a spokeshave, a rasp and sandpaper.

28 Perhaps oddly, even though the case itself was nailed together, the components of the plinth on the Shaker original were assembled with through dovetails. I decided to use that same joinery. Before I cut any dovetails, I numbered components at each corner to ensure that I wouldn't mix them up during the dovetailing process.

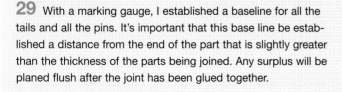

29 With a marking gauge, I established a baseline for all the tails and all the pins. It's important that this base line be established a distance from the end of the part that is slightly greater than the thickness of the parts being joined. Any surplus will be planed flush after the joint has been glued together.

30 After squaring up lines across the end grain of the part on which dovetails would be cut, I sketched in the approximate shapes of the tails and then, with a backsaw, I started saw cuts in the part's end grain. I separate the initial saw cuts from the complete saw cuts in order to better focus myself on starting perpendicular cuts.

31 I then cut the sides of the tails freehand. This results in joinery that is unmistakably hand cut because every dovetail is slightly different than the one beside it.

32 You can see the slight variations in tail shape. Once the parts have been assembled, the eye refuses to register these variations. It's only when you put a bevel square to the tails that you see the differences in angle.

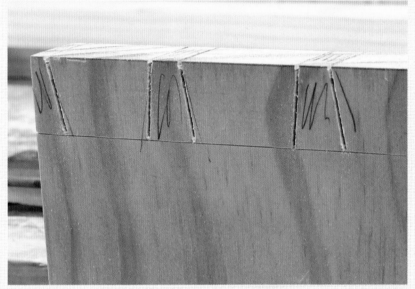

33 I'm removing the bulk of the waste between the tails with a coping saw.

34 After clamping the part to a bit of scrap on my bench top, I clean up the end grain between tails with a paring chisel, working towards the middle from both sides.

35 With a wide paring chisel, I clean up the saw marks of both sides of each tail.

36 To mark the pins, I clamp the pin stock in a vise and lay the tail stock on top of the end grain of the pin stock. Because the pin stock was so long, I cobbled together another little construction to help align the parts for marking.

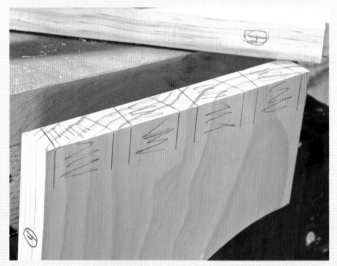

37 I use a sharp pencil to mark the widths of the tails on the end grain of the pin stock.

38 With a try square, I square down to the baseline as shown here. The scribbles indicating waste remind me which side of the line I should cut on.

39 Because the front and back components of the plinth are relatively thin, I stiffened them with a backing board in my vise before I started to cut the joinery.

40 After I've cut out the waste using the same methods I used in Photos 32-34, I did my first trial fit of the joint, gently tapping on the dovetailed component with a soft-headed (and well used) mallet.

41 When I began to get resistance during the trial fit, I tapped off the dovetailed component and looked at the pins. Wherever the fit was too snug, there was evidence of compression and scuffing on the sides of the pin as you see here. With a paring chisel, I removed thin shavings from this and other snug pins, repeating the trial fit and paring process several times until I had what I felt was a close but not too tight fit of tails and pins.

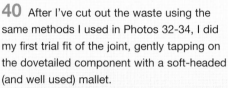
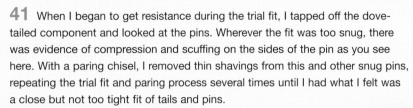

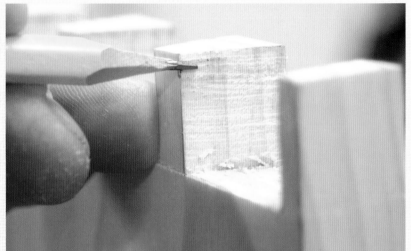

42 Before I glued up the plinth, I first gathered all my gluing materials: glue, glue cup, glue spreading stick, water, mallet, clamp. I also taped cauls to the dovetailed components so that I could apply clamping pressure behind the pins so they will fully seat.

43 After gluing up all mating surfaces, I start the pins in their sockets by gently tapping on the tailed components with a mallet.

44 Once the pins are started on their way, I switch to a pipe clamp which squeezes parts together without the risk of fracture that can occur when parts are driven together with a mallet. In most assembly situations, this is a fairly routine process, but because I was seating tails on the bottom of the plinth where there is no stock connecting the two sides of the parts being joined, I struggled a bit, relying more on a mallet to seat the tails than I would have liked. If I were to build this piece again, I would screw a caul across the bottoms of the feet, so that I could use my pipe clamp to drive the tails home there—without running a risk of breaking anything.

45 After the glue has cured, I plane down the surplus length of all pins and tails with a Lie-Nielson low-angle block plane (which Tom Lie-Nielsen specifically designed for applications like this).

46 Because I didn't have access to the original Canterbury chest, I wasn't sure how the unseen parts were aligned. The understructure of this chest is my design, rather than a reproduction of the original. I decided to glue and screw cleats to the inside of the plinth. The case frame will be attached to these cleats. I'm screwing one of those cleats into place.

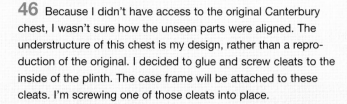

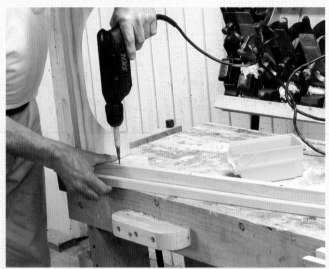

47 I roughed in the half-lap joints for the frame with a stack of dado cutters on my radial arm saw.

48 I then fine-tuned the half-lap joints with a wide shoulder plane.

49 The frame is held together with glue, as well as some countersunk $1/2$" No.6 woodscrews. Notice the framing square which ensures that this frame will be square.

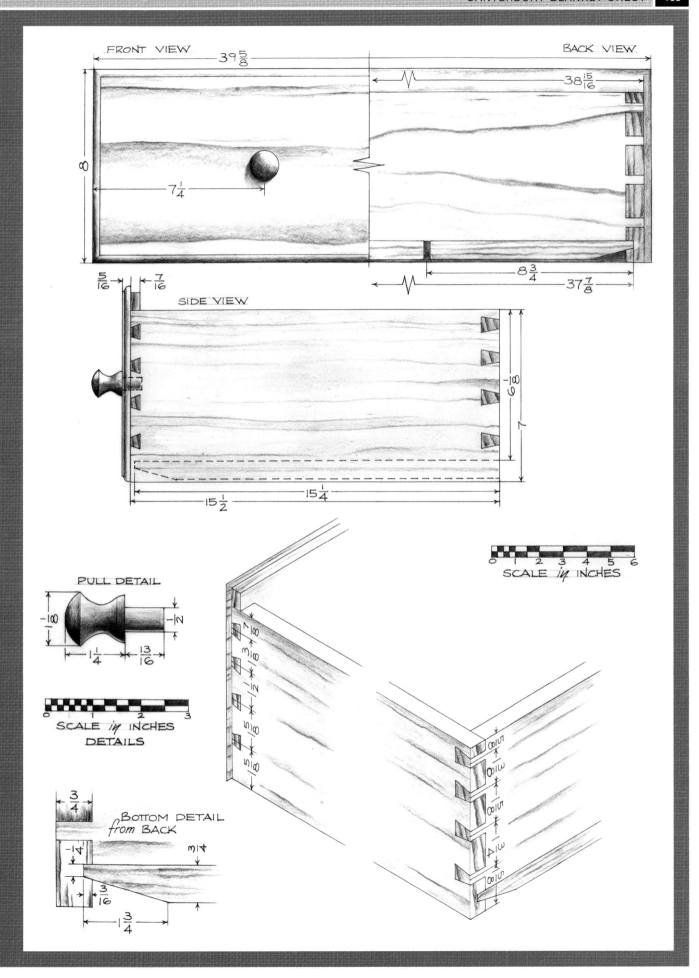

FRONT VIEW

$39\frac{5}{8}$

BACK VIEW

$38\frac{15}{16}$

8

$7\frac{1}{4}$

$8\frac{3}{4}$

$37\frac{7}{8}$

$\frac{5}{16}$ $\frac{7}{16}$

SIDE VIEW

$6\frac{1}{8}$

7

$15\frac{1}{2}$

$15\frac{1}{4}$

PULL DETAIL

$1\frac{1}{8}$ $\frac{1}{2}$

$1\frac{1}{4}$ $\frac{13}{16}$

SCALE in INCHES
0 1 2 3
DETAILS

SCALE in INCHES
0 1 2 3 4 5 6

BOTTOM DETAIL from BACK

$\frac{3}{4}$

$\frac{1}{4}$

$\frac{3}{4}$

$\frac{3}{16}$

$1\frac{3}{4}$

$\frac{7}{8}$

$3\frac{1}{8}$

$1\frac{1}{2}$

$5\frac{5}{8}$

$5\frac{5}{8}$

$\frac{5}{8}$

$\frac{3}{8}$

$\frac{5}{8}$

$\frac{3}{4}$

$\frac{5}{8}$

50 I screwed the frame to the cleats using several 1^1/$_4$" drywall screws.

51 I positioned the chest on the frame and drew a line around its exterior.

52 I then added more cleats, placing their outside edges ^{3}/$_4$" inside the line. (The ^{3}/$_4$" measurement accounts for the ^{3}/$_4$" thickness of the sides of the case.)

53 I joined the case to the plinth with a row of 1^1/$_4$" drywall screws all the way around. (The heads were later concealed by moulding.)

54 Although I profiled mouldings for many years with router bits, I have since turned to moulding planes in large part because they're so much fun to play with. However, I don't mean to suggest that anyone else should make their mouldings for this or any other piece the same way I do (unless, of course, they share my affection for these functional antique planes). Since I do create my mouldings with planes, that's the method I'm going to demonstrate here.

The first task in creating any moulding is selecting a profile that is appropriate for the setting in which you'll place that moulding. That selection process involves considerations of size, as well as aesthetics. Some of the moulding planes in my collection produce profiles only $3/16$" in width, while others produce mouldings over 3" in width, so the first decision you must make is matching profile width to the setting in which the profile will be placed. The selection process might also include considerations of historical accuracy, as the profiles of these moulding planes changed over time, with an individual profile being associated with a specific historical era. This is an issue I addressed at length in the 2008 issue of the *Journal of the Society of American Period Furniture Makers*. Briefly, I would say I rarely worry about the historical accuracy of a particular profile. Instead, if the profile is the right size and if it looks good in the setting I use it.

In my moulding plane cabinet, I keep a small sample of the profile cut by each plane beside that plane. I then simply place that sample in the spot I hope to use it, and if it looks good, that's the profile I use.

If you're new to moulding planes, I'd like to take just a moment to talk about the features of a moulding plane that come into play when you're using it to create mouldings.

First, despite the complexity of the cutting edge on many moulding planes, these planes are quite simple to sharpen. Unless the edge is badly degraded by rust, all that's needed is flattening and polishing the back. This is because the cutting edge is the intersection of two surfaces: the bevel on the front of the iron and the flat on the back of the iron. Working either of these surfaces will result in a sharp edge. This method will work well on a plane you use only occasionally. However, if you use that same plane often enough to require several lappings of the back, those repeated lappings will cause the profile to change significantly enough to interfere with its effective use, which will necessitate a reshaping of the cutting edge.

The shallow step on the right-hand side of the plane in this photo (the step at the bottom of the incised line on the toe of this plane) is the plane's fence which is crowded against the edge of the board being worked. To the left of that fence is the sole's profile which is the reverse of the profile the plane will cut. The strip of material inlaid into the plane's sole is a strip of end-grain boxwood which protects that portion of the plane's sole that is most likely to experience wear. And finally, the narrow flat to the left of the boxing is the depth stop. When that flat strikes the surface of the board being worked, the profile is complete. Also, notice the crossing lines incised on the toe (front) of the plane. These are called spring lines. They must be aligned with true vertical and true horizontal when the plane is in use. When they are aligned in this way, the plane is being used at the correct angle.

A WORD ABOUT MOULDING PROFILES

In the 19th century, every cabinet shop had a rack of moulding planes. Most of these were hollows and rounds which, when used in conjunction with rabbet planes and snipe bills could create an almost infinite variety of moulding profiles. In addition, cabinet shops nearly always had a collection of dedicated planes designed to cut very specific moulding shapes.

For example, when a cabinetmaker needed a moulded shape to run around the lid of a blanket chest (like the Canterbury blanket chest appearing on page 90 or the Union Village blanket chest appearing on page 138), the craftsman simply picked a tool from his rack of dedicated planes that cut a profile appropriate in size and shape for that application.

With the exception of high-style shops in metropolitan areas like New York and Philadelphia, craftsmen rarely concerned themselves with acquiring profiles that were exact matches for profiles used by other craftsmen making the same kinds of pieces. All that was necessary was a plane capable of cutting a profile that would fit into a prescribed space and produce, in that space, an appealing clutter of shadow lines.

Some modern makers who reproduce period and Shaker forms find it difficult to work in such a way. They feel their mouldings must be exact matches for the mouldings they see on the originals they're reproducing. But in the real world in which our woodworking ancestors worked, few craftsmen insisted on such a slavish approach to moulding profiles. Instead, they simply chose from the profiles that the dedicated planes in their shop could produce.

And that's my advice for any reader who might be looking to reproduce any of the forms in this book. If you don't have a moulding plane or a router bit or a shaper cutter that will create the exact profile you see here, relax. Look at what you have on hand. Choose a profiling tool that will work in that application, and enjoy the form that results.

Although it may seem counter-intuitive, that is the most historically faithful manner in which to work.

This is one of my moulding and joinery plane cabinets. On the top left, I have a collection of dado planes, each cutting a trench of a different width. In the top center, I have a pair of moving fillisters that see a lot of use. On the middle shelf I have a row of moulding planes. Most of these are accompanied by a short sample of the moulding (on each plane's left). These samples are important because they make it possible for me to test moulding shapes in the situation for which I'm considering that shape. On the bottom right, I have a couple of moulding sandwiches assembled from profiles cut by several different planes. Even if you prefer to create mouldings with routers, rather than moulding planes, a shelf of samples presenting the profile cut by each of your router bits can simplify the process of choosing a profile for a specific situation.

55 In this photo, you can see that the profile is nearly completed. Notice that the fence is crowded against the edge of the board. Notice also the slight gap between the depth stop and the surface of the stock I'm working. When that gap is closed, the profile will be complete.

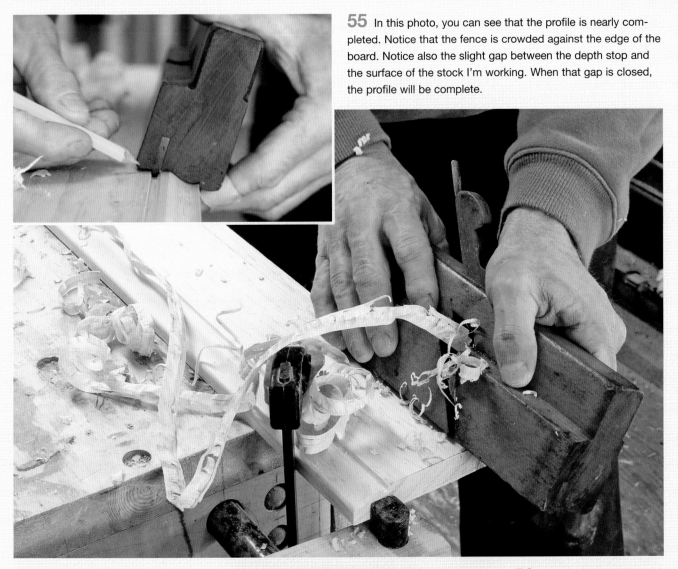

56 Because it's so difficult to work narrow strips of wood with a moulding plane (or with a router), I mould edges and then cut the moulding from the wider board. In some cases, I do what you see here: I mould both edges and cut them from the wider board.

57 I decided to nail the moulding onto the plinth. It would have been awkward to get good clamping pressure on the shaped, top surface of the moulding.

58 With any hand-made moulding, there are slight variations where two pieces come together at a miter. These variations required a little touching up with sandpaper.

59 After I ripped out the front, back and sides of the drawer, using a stack of dado cutters on my table saw I plowed the grooves in them for the drawer's bottom. I then moved the fence and used the same dado cutters to cut the rabbet on the two ends and top of the drawer front.

60 Because it's difficult to cut a profile with a hand plane across the grain on the end of a drawer front, I chose to use a $1/2$"-roundover router bit for that purpose.

61 The through dovetails at the back of the drawer are laid out and cut just like the through dovetails on the plinth. The half-blind dovetails at the front of the drawer, however, are a little different. First, I scored the baseline for these dovetails—a distance from the end of the board equal to the depth of the rabbet on the back of the drawer. After I cut the tails, I clamped the drawer front in my vise as shown. I then laid the tails over the rabbet on the back of the drawer front and marked the tails as shown.

62 I reversed the drawer front in my vise, and with my try square, I squared down to the baseline on the back of the drawer front. The scribbles indicate waste.

63 Next I carefully made starting cuts with my backsaw just a hair inside the waste areas.

64 With various bench chisels, I chopped out the waste between pins to create the sockets that would receive the tails.

65 During the final dry fit, the dovetails should fit into their sockets deeply enough so that there is surplus length on the pins that can be planed down after final assembly.

66 I raised a panel for the drawer bottom the same way I raised the panels for the chest bottoms in Photos 16-17, with one small difference: Drawer bottoms only need to have bevels planed on three sides since the back isn't fit into a groove. I cut a pair of notches on the back edge of the drawer bottom. After sliding the drawer bottom into its grooves in the drawer sides and the back face of the drawer front, I secured the drawer bottom by turning a pair of screws, inside the notches, up into the bottom edge of the drawer back.

67 I turned the drawer knobs using these two tools. With the narrow skew chisel on the left, I turned the crowned top of the knob, and with the $1/4$" fingernail gouge on the right, I turned the cove. (The tenon on the bottom was turned with a wide butt chisel laid bevel side down on my toolrest.)

68 After drilling the through-mortises for the knob tenons using my drill press, I notched the tenons and fit a wedge into each notch. Then I glued the tenon, wedge and notch. After inserting the tenon into its mortise, I tapped the wedge into place with a hammer. Later, after the glue had dried, I sawed off the surplus length of the tenon on the inside of the drawer.

69 After screwing cleats to the underside of the lid to reduce cupping, I cut a saw-blade wide groove in both ends of the lid to receive the spline that would fasten the moulding to the end of the lid. (Even though I wasn't ready to attach mouldings, these grooves needed to be cut before I attached the lid hardware.)

70 With a marking gauge, I set the depth of the hinge mortise on the back of the chest. This depth should be equal to half of the thickness of the closed hinge measured at the pin.

71 I then began to nibble away at the mortise using a bench chisel as shown.

72 When I reached the right depth, I cleaned up the bottom of the mortise by paring it smooth.

73 After installing both hinges in their mortises on the chest back, I put the lid in its proper position and marked the locations of the hinge mortises on the back edge of the lid.

74 I cut the moulded edge that will run around the lid using a thumbnail plane, operated in the manner described in Photos No.54- No.56. I then sliced off the width of the final mouldings from the wide board.

75 I cut saw-blade wide grooves on the inside edges of the two pieces of moulding that would be fastened to the ends of the lid. (No groove is necessary for the moulding on the front of the lid because that can be edge-glued to the front of the lid.)

76 Before I attached any moulding to the lid, I did a little sanding on the lid to remove a couple of areas of tearout I hadn't been able to clean up with my smoothing plane.

77 I then created tiny bevels on the front and both ends of the top outside edges of the lid to better mark the union of lid and moulded edge. I created similar bevels on the top, inside edges of the moulding pieces.

78 I often use my table saw and miter gauge to cut miters as I'm doing here.

79 A shooting board and a miter plane will allow you to create tight, clean miters.

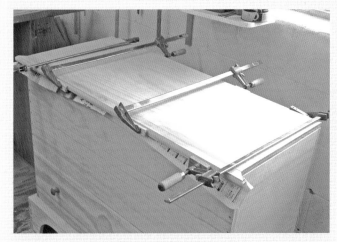

80 The moulding on the front edge of the lid doesn't require splines. It can simply be edge-glued in place.

81 I made my splines by running a small cherry board through my thickness planer repeatedly until I achieved a thickness that was reasonably, but not excessively snug in the saw kerfs made by the carbide blade on my table saw. The "reasonably, but not excessively snug" description is a little vague, but it is accurate. If the splines are too thin, the moulding won't be held tightly to the ends of the lid; however, if the spline is too thick, you won't be able to get the splines fully seated during glue up. If you're not sure about this thickness, run some splines and test their fit.

The strength of these splines results from the fact that their grain runs perpendicular to the grain of the moulding in which they fit, and it's imperative that you fit your splines in that way. If you fit them with the grain running parallel to the grain of the moulding, the moulding will break off at the first sign of stress.

The lid will shrink across its width over time; therefore, the spline can't be glued along the full length of the moulding. I glued only 5"-6" of the section closest to the miter. That will keep the miter joint tight. The movement resulting from shrinkage will take place at the unglued end of the moulding.

82 The final moulding is a transitional profile that fits around the top of the case, as shown.

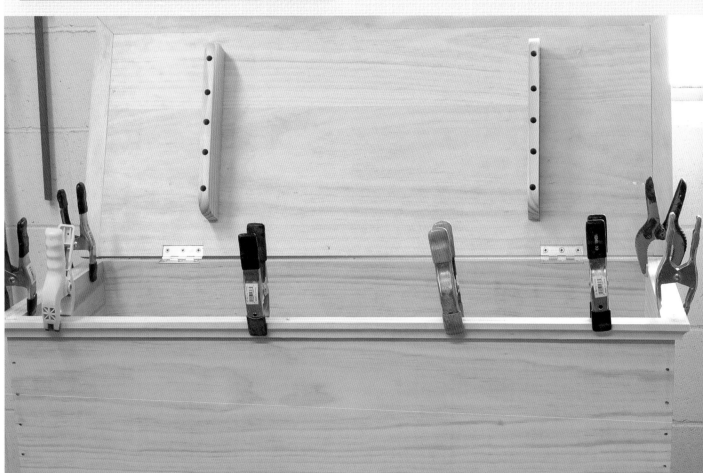

Inside edge
of chest end

5/8

1 9/16

83 Unfortunately, most hardware is sold without a single word of installation instructions. That was true for the hinges, the lid stays and for the lock I used on this piece. That omission is frustrating enough for someone like me who's been installing hardware for forty years — I can only imagine how frustrating it must be for a woodworker just getting started.

This photo spells out the measurements for the four mounting screws used in mounting the lid stay. Sometimes the screws that come with these stays are a bit too long for ¾" material. If yours are too long, simply touch the tips of the screws to a rotating grinding wheel to remove a bit of length. (I had to do that with all of the screws I used for my two lid stays.)

(I found both the right-handed and left-handed lid stays at our local Lowe's. They were sold in unmarked plastic bags, so I'm not sure who the manufacturer is. They appear to be exact matches for other curved, lid stays I've used on other pieces over the years, so I'm guessing that all were made by the same manufacturer.)

84 I would have installed the rest of my hardware before I applied any finish, but in the case of this chest, I had failed to order my lock soon enough, so I went ahead with final sanding and finishing.

85 The completed chest is ready for finishing.

86 Because I had opted for a two-tone paint job, I masked those surfaces that would not be receiving color before I applied my primer.

87 I began the installation of the lock by marking the mortise for the lock's (brass chest lock CL-5 in the Horton Brasses catalog) mechanism on the inside of the chest's front.

88 The lock mechanism mortise has two parts: A shallow mortise for the brass plate on the top of the mechanism case and a thicker, deeper mortise for the case itself. Here, I'm nibbling my way down into the deeper mortise.

89 This is the completed mortise ready for the installation of the lock. Notice that the round hole and notch for the key tooth have been cut. These should be cut from the front side to eliminate the possibility of any splinters breaking out on the front side of the through mortises. Also, you should use a Forstner bit rather than a twist bit for drilling the round hole because twist bits tear up the wood around the mortise.

90 The lock wouldn't close the first time I tried it because of two little bits of wood inside the mortises in the lock works that receive the posts from the strike plate, so I had to remove the works and create two small additional mortises.

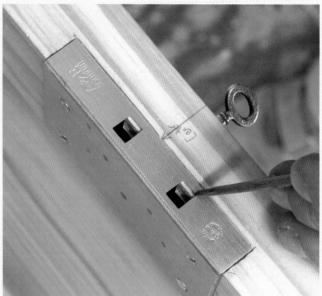

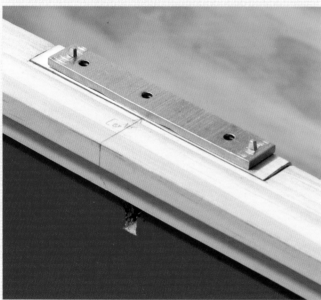

91 Probably the fussiest part of any chest lock installation is the alignment of the strike plate on the underside of the lid so that the two parts of the lock come together as they should. Fortunately, lock manufacturers understand this so they add an alignment feature to the back of the strike plate—although they don't include any directions to explain how that feature works. In this photo, the strike plate is locked into the mechanism case. Notice the two brass nubs sticking up on the back of that strike plate. When I close the lid on those nubs, they will leave impressions on the underside of the lid telling me where the strike plate should be located.

92 Here, you can see how the back side of the strike plate matches up with the impressions made by the two nubs.

PROJECT THREE

YELLOW WOOD BOX
FROM SABBATHDAY LAKE

Several years ago, on a trip to Maine to interview toolmaker Tom Lie-
Nielsen and two furniture makers on behalf of *Woodcraft* magazine,
I stopped at the Sabbathday Lake Shaker community in rural Maine.
Although this community is not as well known as Pleasant Hill,
Kentucky, or Lebanon, New York, it is the only Shaker community that
still has a population of practicing Shakers, although that population is
quite small.

The museum director was kind enough to take me on a tour of the
museum's collection, which is larger than you might expect because this
community became the repository for the goods shipped from other
Shaker communities in the region as those communities closed in the
early 20th century due to declining populations.

During my tour, I measured two pieces, both of which struck me as
particularly appealing forms: A little peg-leg candlestand and the yellow
wood box you see here.

Because the construction of this box is, in many ways, similar to the
construction of the Canterbury chest in the previous chapter, I'm not
going to attempt an exhaustive documentation of the construction process. Instead, I'll be referring you to the previous chapter for information
on how this piece can be built.

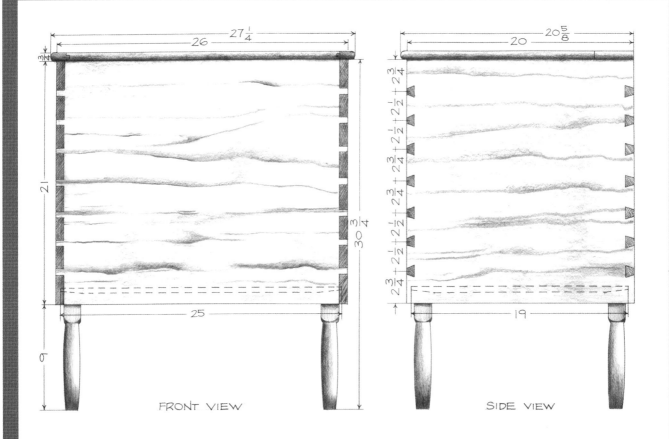

27 1/4
26
3/4
21
30 3/4
25
9

FRONT VIEW

20 5/8
20
2 3/4
2 1/2
2 1/2
2 3/4
2 3/4
2 1/2
2 1/2
2 3/4
2 1/2
2 3/4
19

SIDE VIEW

0 1 2 3 4 5 6 7 8 9 10 11 12
SCALE in INCHES

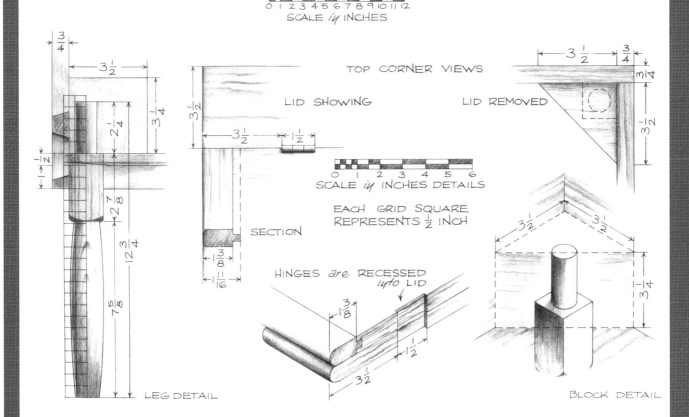

3/4
3 1/2
2 1/4
3 1/4
1/2
1
2 7/8
12 3/4
7 5/8

LEG DETAIL

3 1/2
3 1/2
3 1/2
1 1/2
1 3/8
1 11/16

SECTION

TOP CORNER VIEWS

LID SHOWING   LID REMOVED

3 1/2   3/4
3/4
3 1/2

0 1 2 3 4 5 6
SCALE in INCHES DETAILS

EACH GRID SQUARE
REPRESENTS 1/2 INCH

HINGES are RECESSED into LID

3/8
1/2
3 1/2

3 1/2   3 1/2
3 1/4

BLOCK DETAIL

1 We sometimes forget the Shakers' love of color. Here, we see the original wood box in its current location in the Sabbathday Lake museum where it stands in front of a wall decorated with blue base, casing and chair rail.

2 The lid is hinged to a strip on the back which is nailed to the top edges of the sides and back.

3 This close-up of the original box shows the head of a cut nail which is working its way loose. It also shows the battered surfaces of this 150-year-old antique. In my reproduction of this original, I used several distressing techniques to mimic the texture of this battered surface.

4 Inside the original chest, you can see a narrow strip, triangular in cross section, in the inside corner. Because I couldn't figure out the purpose of this strip I didn't include it in my reproduction.

5 One of the difficulties of measuring antiques is determining the nature of the hidden details. I'm certain there is a tenon at the top of this leg, although there's no angle that will allow me to see it. What I'm not certain of is how long that tenon is. I do know, however, that there is nothing other than the triangular-in-cross-section strip in the bottom inside corners of the box. This suggests that the tenon is only long enough to penetrate the bottom of the box, that is unless the tenon is thin enough in diameter to be concealed in the strip. As you'll see, I opted for a different interior. I put a hefty glue block into each corner and ran a thick leg tenon up into the underside of each block.

6 At the time I was building this box, I was experimenting with an unusual style of jointing plane: a transitional plane with an attached fence that simplifies the accurate jointing of edges.

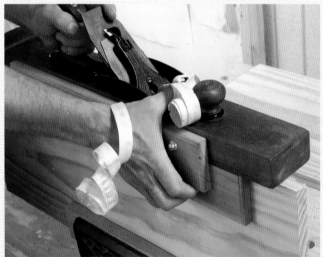

7 The process of gluing up the six panels is just like the process I documented in the Canterbury chest chapter.

8 Because I was trying to reproduce the texture of the original, I used smoothing planes equipped with irons having a slight radius ground across their width. These allowed me to create gentle hollows on the surface of the panels. You may not see them when you look at the piece, but you will feel them when you run your hand across its surfaces.

9 Using the method I described in the Canterbury chest chapter, I'm using a jack plane to create a raised panel for the box bottom.

10 The biggest difference between this box and the Canterbury chest is the method by which the corners are joined. In the case of the Canterbury chest, those corners are joined using cut nails. In the case of this wood box, the corners are joined with through dovetails. I cut these dovetails using the same process I described for cutting the dovetails in the plinth of the Canterbury chest.

11 This is one of the legs I turned for this box. Notice the long tenon which will penetrate completely through the bottom and then rise into the big glue blocks in each corner of the box.

12 Here you can see one of those glue blocks. To install the block, I glued the three contact surfaces and pressed the block in place, holding it there for about 45 seconds.

13 Before I did any distressing, I created a surface that looked—I think—much like the surface of original box looked when it was brand new. Because the yellow pigment on the original was semi-transparent, I used a spray-on yellow without a primer. The absence of a primer meant that the color wouldn't cover well and would, in fact, allow the wood to show through, just like the paint on the original. I then sanded the surfaces smooth.

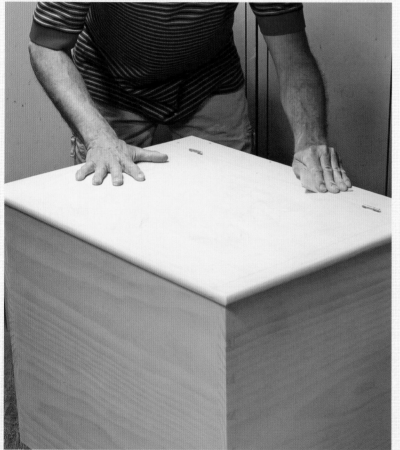

14 I've never before attempted finish quite this distressed, and I have to admit I had fun with the process. I knew I couldn't reproduce the exact surfaces of the original. What I tried to do, instead, is to mimic the character of that original surface. These are some of the products I used in that attempt.

First, I used files and rasps to soften the sharp corners. Then I battered the surfaces of the box with a sock containing a variety of "distressers". First I filled the sock with nails and whacked the entire surface. Then I removed the nails from the sock and replaced them with bolts. Then I switched to marbles. I then finished up with a few whacks using my mallet.

The original had can rings on the top (see Photo No.2) so I wiped a bit of pigment on the bottoms of the two cans you see here and left some can prints. The original also had a lot of dirt ground into its surfaces, so I mixed up a thick slurry of mud, driveway sand and water and rubbed it over all the surfaces with a rag.

I had expected to be done at that point, but when I stepped back and looked at the box, it still looked like something new that had been artificially aged. I decided this was because the color was too homogenous, lacking the variations that come with age. So my next step was to take a water-based craft paint a good bit darker than the yellow already on the box and begin working that paint over the surfaces with a rag, leaving some areas with heavy paint and others with very light paint, in this way creating a more varied surface. The last step was a coat of brush-on-wipe-off polyurethane to give my dirty surface a bit of protection.

PROJECT FOUR

SMALL CHEST

The six-board chest (composed of four sides a top and bottom) is a country (and Shaker) standard. This piece represents a variation on that standard in two respects. The grain
is aligned vertically in the ends so they can extend below the
bottom of the chest to raise it from the ground. The top is a
break from tradition with a thin moulding running along all
four edges.

While many of the pieces appearing in this book require
a week or more of time to construct, this tiny chest, with its
simple bandsawn profiles and its simple nailed construction,
could be built in a single day.

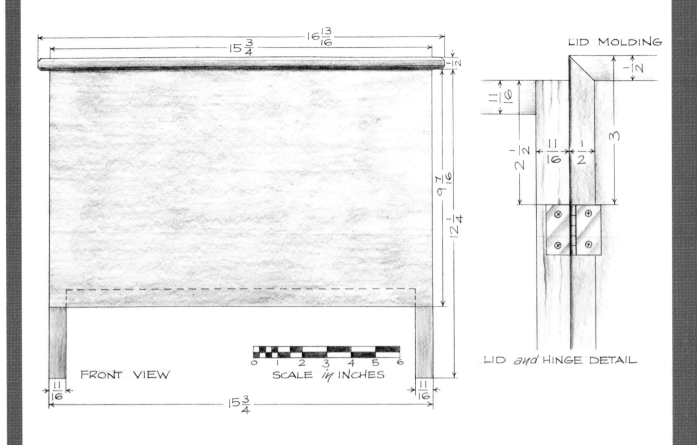

FRONT VIEW

SCALE *in* INCHES

LID MOLDING

LID *and* HINGE DETAIL

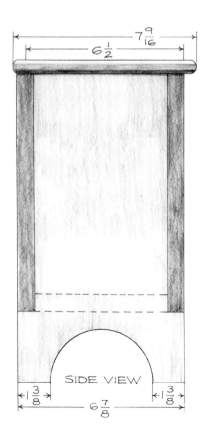

SIDE VIEW

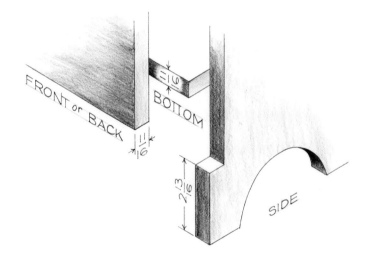

FRONT or BACK

BOTTOM

SIDE

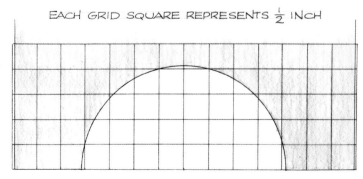

EACH GRID SQUARE REPRESENTS $\frac{1}{2}$ INCH

1 After flattening and straightening my stock, I ripped the components to width and cut them to length. I then laid out the band saw cuts on the two end panels. As you see here, I marked the half circle between the foot with a compass.

2 I'm illustrating the amount of surplus length I ensured for the two side panels so I would have material to plane flush in order to achieve a tight fit and to remove the end-grain tearout left behind by a cross-cut saw. The amount of surplus length is too small to be measured or marked. I simply establish it by sliding my fingers over the intersection of side panel and end.

3 I used a Lie-Nielson low-angle jack plane to level the end grain surplus of the side panels. Notice the clamping arrangement I created to allow me to hold the case while I planed. First, I fixed a narrow board in my end vise. I then clamped the case to that board with a pair of short bar clamps.

4 After creating a radius on a wide board using the three-pencil-lines technique, I ripped the moulding to its final width and nailed it around the lid's center panel. The lid will likely shrink a bit across its width over time, but because the center panel is relatively narrow, that shrinkage isn't likely to be enough to cause problems, and, unlike glue, nails give laterally, so a small amount of shrinkage won't cause the mouldings to pop off.

5 I filled the nail holes with putty and sanded it flush with the surface.

6 After masking around the top (so I could finish the interior natural), I applied a latex primer, then a latex topcoat.

PROJECT ONE

THE HAMLIN CUPBOARD

Only a handful of Pleasant Hill pieces were signed by their makers. Perhaps this focus on self (as a signature could imply) was antithetical to the communal nature of life as a Shaker. This piece, however, is signed, bearing the name Charles Hamlin and is dated: "Jan 30th 1877".

The construction can be divided into two parts: A cupboard above accessed by three large doors and chest of drawers below broken into four large drawers. Like most Pleasant Hill chests of drawers, the base of this unit is assembled using post-and-panel construction for the ends, with the drawer rails tenoned into the posts. The four posts terminate in simple tapered feet, without any detail to mark the transition from the square upper section to the turned lower section. The two outside doors on the upper cabinet are hinged to the sides of the case while the center door is hinged to a stile that represents the only framing element on the front of the cupboard.

The division of the cupboard into three doors rather than two or four is unusual. A cabinet-maker's natural inclination might be to use two wide doors, each mirroring the width of the rack of drawers below. Or, perhaps four narrow doors, broken into two pairs, one above each rack of drawers. The maker of this piece opted for three doors, even though the decision necessitated the inclusion of a single off-center stile.

He may have decided that two very wide doors would place too much strain on the doors' mortise-and-tenon joinery, and he may have decided that four very narrow doors would make the upper cupboard too cluttered with panels. But I like to think that he opted for three doors because it provides such an appealing counterpoint to the two racks of drawers below.

The cupboard is surmounted with an extremely wide cove moulding, anchored in place with a series of glue blocks. There is also a much smaller moulding at the waist where the upper and lower portions come together.

Larrie Curry, the Pleasant Hill museum director, says that some experts doubt the 1877 date, believing that the piece was built much earlier.

One of the largest free-standing pieces in the furniture collection of the restored Shaker community at Pleasant Hill, Kentucky, the Charles Hamlin cupboard over chest of drawers represents the highest standards of Shaker design and craftsmanship.

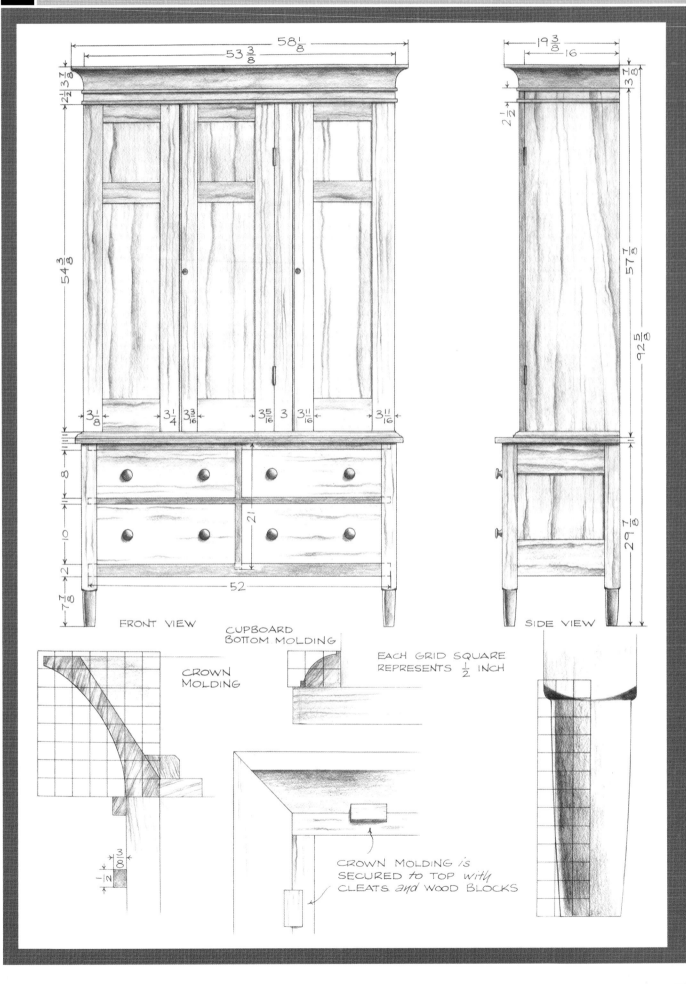

FRONT VIEW

SIDE VIEW

CUPBOARD
BOTTOM MOLDING

EACH GRID SQUARE
REPRESENTS $\frac{1}{2}$ INCH

CROWN
MOLDING

CROWN MOLDING is
SECURED to TOP with
CLEATS and WOOD BLOCKS

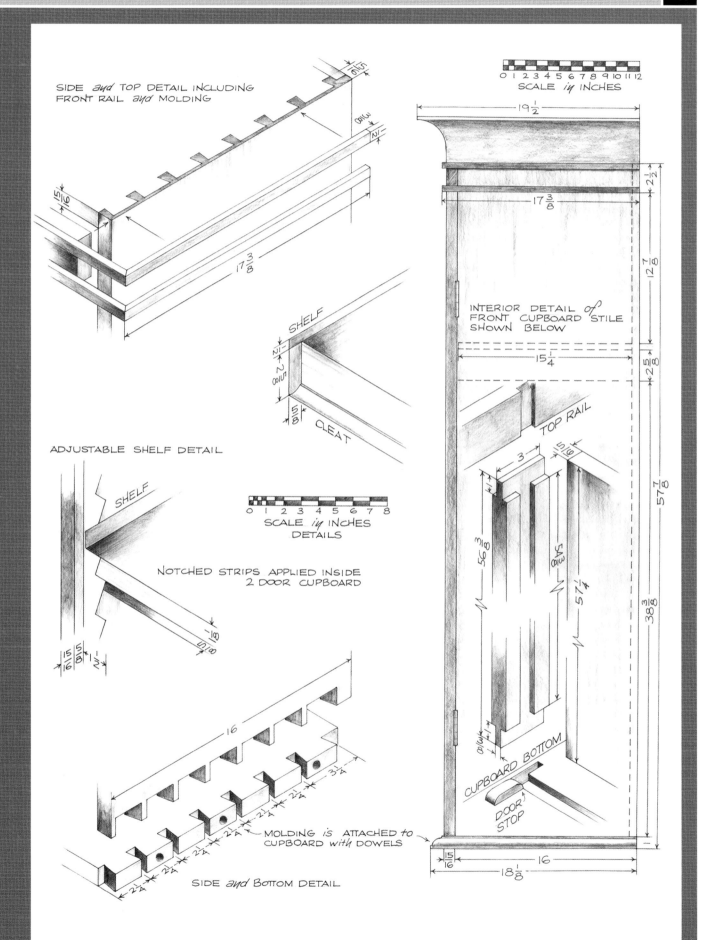

SIDE *and* TOP DETAIL INCLUDING
FRONT RAIL *and* MOLDING

SCALE *in* INCHES

SHELF

CLEAT

ADJUSTABLE SHELF DETAIL

SHELF

SCALE *in* INCHES
DETAILS

NOTCHED STRIPS APPLIED INSIDE
2 DOOR CUPBOARD

MOLDING *is* ATTACHED *to*
CUPBOARD *with* DOWELS

SIDE *and* BOTTOM DETAIL

INTERIOR DETAIL *of*
FRONT CUPBOARD STILE
SHOWN BELOW

TOP RAIL

CUPBOARD BOTTOM

DOOR
STOP

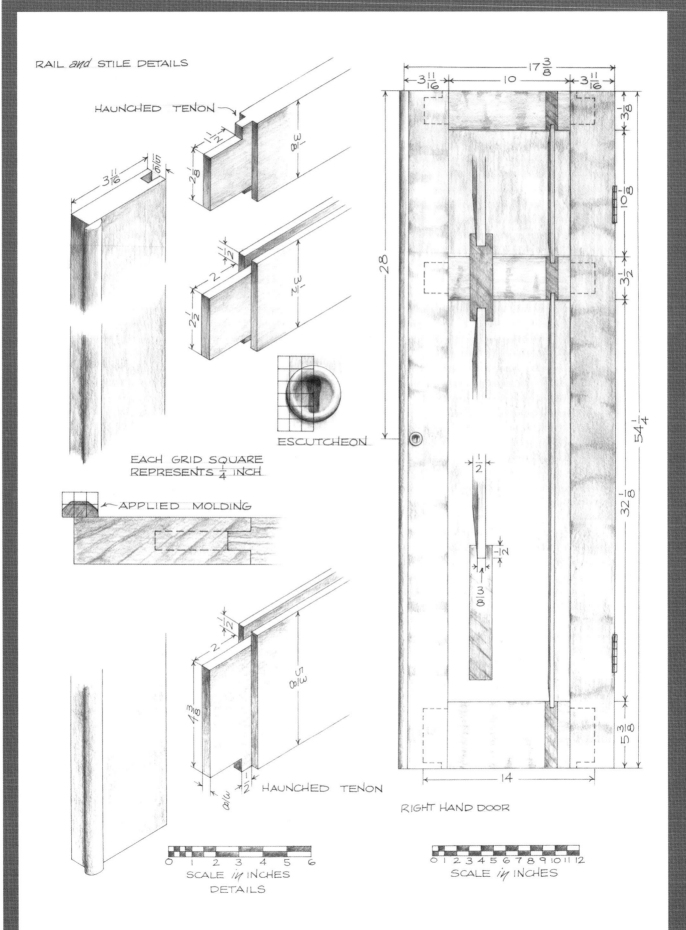

RAIL *and* STILE DETAILS

HAUNCHED TENON

$3\frac{11}{16}$

$\frac{5}{16}$

$1\frac{1}{2}$

$2\frac{1}{8}$

$3\frac{1}{8}$

$\frac{1}{2}$

2

$2\frac{1}{2}$

$3\frac{1}{2}$

ESCUTCHEON

EACH GRID SQUARE
REPRESENTS $\frac{1}{4}$ INCH

APPLIED MOLDING

$\frac{1}{2}$

2

$2\frac{1}{2}$

$4\frac{3}{8}$

$5\frac{3}{8}$

$\frac{1}{2}$

$\frac{3}{8}$

HAUNCHED TENON

SCALE *in* INCHES
DETAILS

0 1 2 3 4 5 6

RIGHT HAND DOOR

$17\frac{3}{8}$

$3\frac{11}{16}$

10

$3\frac{11}{16}$

$\frac{3}{8}$

$10\frac{1}{8}$

$3\frac{1}{2}$

28

$54\frac{1}{4}$

$32\frac{1}{8}$

$\frac{1}{2}$

$\frac{1}{2}$

$\frac{3}{8}$

$5\frac{3}{8}$

14

SCALE *in* INCHES

0 1 2 3 4 5 6 7 8 9 10 11 12

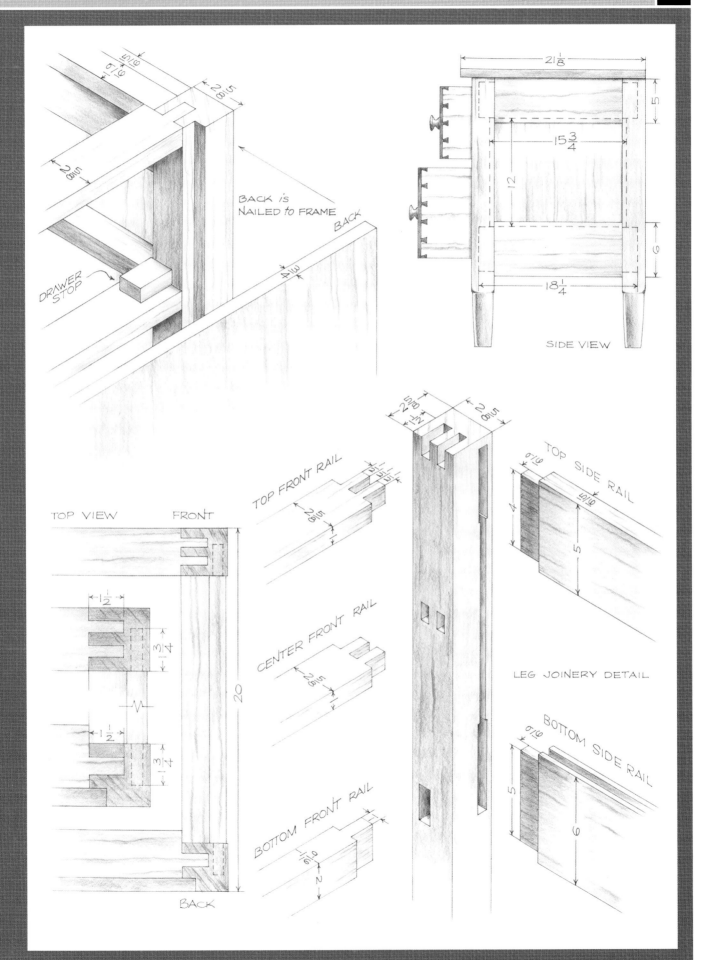

DRAWER STOP

BACK is NAILED to FRAME

BACK

SIDE VIEW

TOP VIEW   FRONT

TOP FRONT RAIL

CENTER FRONT RAIL

BOTTOM FRONT RAIL

TOP SIDE RAIL

LEG JOINERY DETAIL

BOTTOM SIDE RAIL

BACK

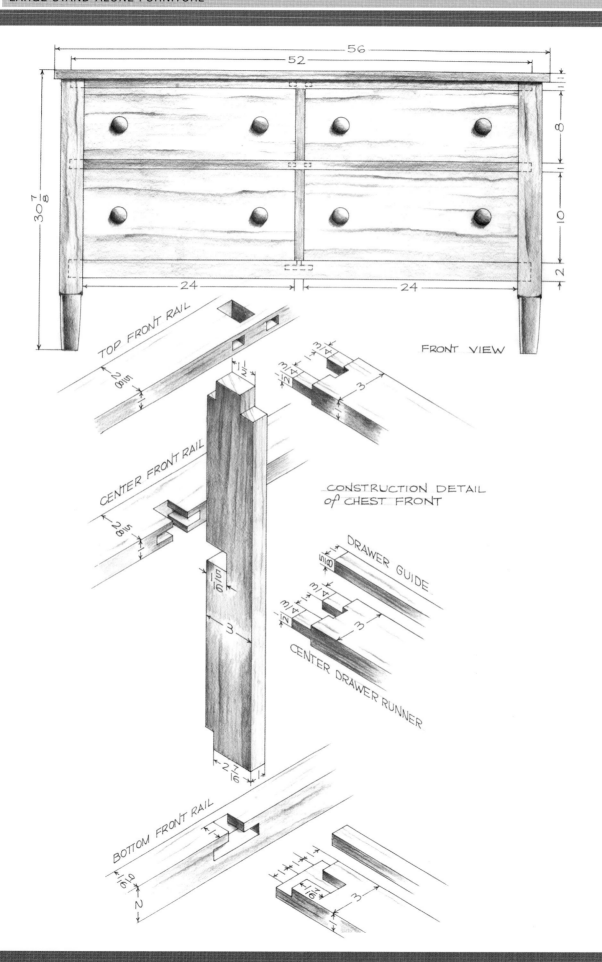

FRONT VIEW

TOP FRONT RAIL

CENTER FRONT RAIL

CONSTRUCTION DETAIL
of CHEST FRONT

DRAWER GUIDE

CENTER DRAWER RUNNER

BOTTOM FRONT RAIL

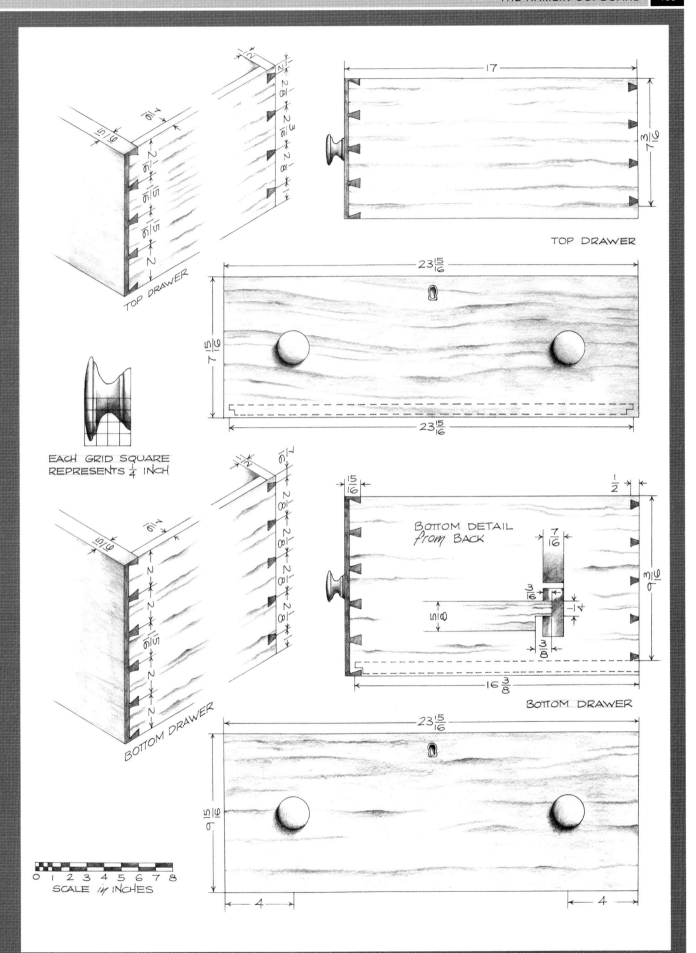

TOP DRAWER

TOP DRAWER

EACH GRID SQUARE
REPRESENTS $\frac{1}{4}$ INCH

BOTTOM DRAWER

BOTTOM DETAIL
from BACK

BOTTOM DRAWER

SCALE *in* INCHES

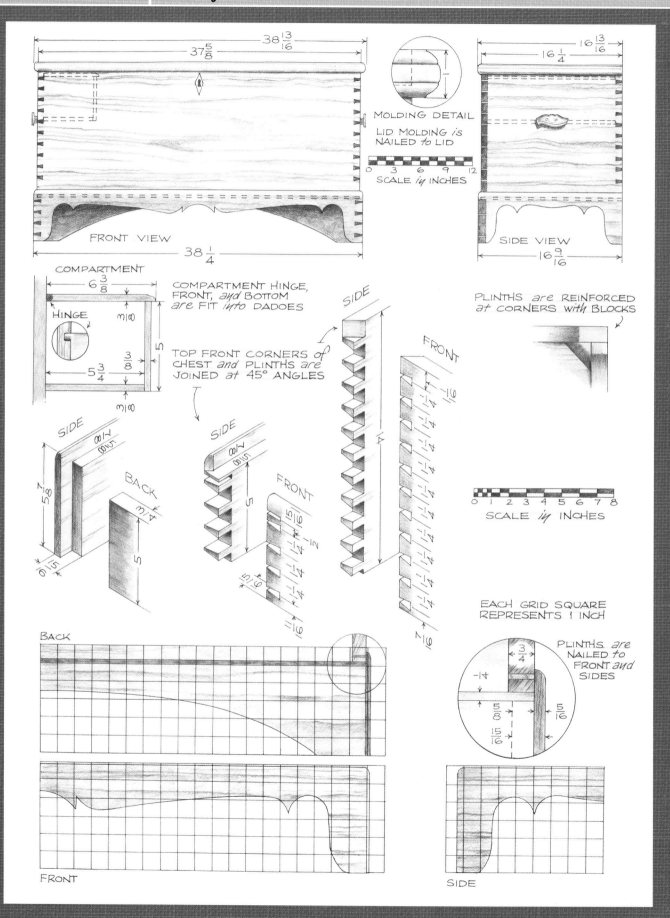

FRONT VIEW

$38\frac{13}{16}$

$37\frac{5}{8}$

$38\frac{1}{4}$

MOLDING DETAIL

LID MOLDING *is*
NAILED *to* LID

SCALE *in* INCHES
0   3   6   9   12

SIDE VIEW

$16\frac{13}{16}$

$16\frac{1}{4}$

$16\frac{9}{16}$

COMPARTMENT

$6\frac{3}{8}$

HINGE

$5\frac{3}{4}$

$\frac{3}{8}$

5

COMPARTMENT HINGE,
FRONT, *and* BOTTOM
are FIT *into* DADOES

TOP FRONT CORNERS *of*
CHEST *and* PLINTHS *are*
JOINED *at* 45° ANGLES

PLINTHS *are* REINFORCED
at CORNERS *with* BLOCKS

SIDE

FRONT

BACK

$5\frac{7}{8}$

$\frac{3}{4}$

5

SIDE

FRONT

SCALE *in* INCHES
0 1 2 3 4 5 6 7 8

EACH GRID SQUARE
REPRESENTS 1 INCH

PLINTHS *are*
NAILED *to*
FRONT *and*
SIDES

$\frac{3}{4}$

$\frac{5}{8}$

$\frac{5}{16}$

$\frac{15}{16}$

BACK

FRONT

SIDE

PROJECT TWO

UNION VILLAGE BLANKET CHEST

This walnut blanket chest is in the collection of Shaker materials at the Warren County Museum in Lebanon, Ohio.

The plinth of this chest is a near-perfect match of the scroll on the base of a chest of drawers in the museum, identified as originating at Union Village, signed and dated Daniel Sering, November 9, 1827, who became a Shaker in the first decade of the nineteenth century and died in 1870.

The ornate handles suggested a worldly origin, but it's impossible, without documenta-tion, to say if a piece was from a Shaker shop or a shop in the World ten miles from the Shaker community.

Late in the Shaker movement, furniture makers were incorporating "fancy" features that had been earlier prohibited by Shaker law. I believe this blanket chest is a later piece.

The hardware and moulding profiles belong to a later era and the chest looks almost show-room new. It's likely this chest was built in the late 19th century.

suppliers

ADAMS & KENNEDY —
THE WOOD SOURCE
6178 Mitch Owen Rd.
P.O. Box 700
Manotick, ON
Canada K4M 1A6
613-822-6800
www.wood-source.com
Wood supply

ADJUSTABLE CLAMP COMPANY
404 N. Armour St.
Chicago, IL 60622
312-666-0640
www.adjustableclamp.com
Clamps and woodworking tools

B&Q
Portswood House
1 Hampshire Corporate Park
Chandlers Ford
Eastleigh
Hampshire, England SO53
3YX
0845 609 6688
www.diy.com
Woodworking tools, supplies and hardware

BUSY BEE TOOLS
130 Great Gulf Dr.
Concord, ON
Canada L4K 5W1
1-800-461-2879
www.busybeetools.com
Woodworking tools and supplies

CONSTANTINE'S WOOD CENTER
OF FLORIDA
1040 E. Oakland Park Blvd.
Fort Lauderdale, FL 33334
800-443-9667
www.constantines.com
Tools, woods, veneers, hardware

FRANK PAXTON LUMBER
COMPANY
5701 W. 66th St.
Chicago, IL 60638
800-323-2203
www.paxtonwood.com
Wood, hardware, tools, books

THE HOME DEPOT
2455 Paces Ferry Rd. NW
Atlanta, GA 30339
800-430-3376 (U.S.)
800-628-0525 (Canada)
www.homedepot.com
Woodworking tools, supplies and hardware

KLINGSPOR ABRASIVES INC.
2555 Tate Blvd. SE
Hickory, N.C. 28602
800-645-5555
www.klingspor.com
Sandpaper of all kinds

LEE VALLEY TOOLS LTD.
P.O. Box 1780
Ogdensburg, NY 13669-6780
800-871-8158 (U.S.)
800-267-8767 (Canada)
www.leevalley.com
Woodworking tools and hardware

LOWE'S COMPANIES, INC.
P.O. Box 1111
North Wilkesboro, NC 28656
800-445-6937
www.lowes.com
Woodworking tools, supplies and hardware

MICROPLANE
2401 E. 16th St.
Russellville, AR 72802
800-555-2767
www.us.microplane.com/
Rotary shaper and other wood-shaping tools

ROCKLER WOODWORKING AND
HARDWARE
4365 Willow Dr.
Medina, MN 55340
800-279-4441
www.rockler.com
Woodworking tools, hardware and books

TOOL TREND LTD.
140 Snow Blvd. Unit 1
Concord, ON
Canada L4K 4C1
416-663-8665
Woodworking tools and hardware

TREND MACHINERY & CUTTING
TOOLS LTD.
Odhams Trading Estate
St. Albans Rd.
Watford
Hertfordshire, U.K.
WD24 7TR
01923 224657
www.trendmachinery.co.uk
Woodworking tools and hardware

VAUGHAN & BUSHNELL MFG. CO.
P. O. Box 390
Hebron, IL 60034
815-648-2446
www.vaughanmfg.com
Hammers and other tools

WATERLOX COATINGS
908 Meech Ave.
Cleveland, OH 44105
800-321-0377
www.waterlox.com
Finishing supplies

WOODCRAFT SUPPLY LLC
1177 Rosemar Rd.
P.O. Box 1686
Parkersburg, WV 26102
800-535-4482
www.woodcraft.com
Woodworking hardware

WOODWORKER'S HARDWARE
P.O. Box 180
Sauk Rapids, MN 56379-0180
800-383-0130
www.wwhardware.com
Woodworking hardware

WOODWORKER'S SUPPLY
1108 N. Glenn Rd.
Casper, WY 82601
800-645-9292
http://woodworker.com
Woodworking tools and accessories, finishing supplies, books and plans

index

More great titles from Popular Woodworking and Betterway books!

PLEASANT HILL SHAKER FURNITURE

By Kerry Pierce

Take a virtual tour through one of the remaining shaker communities. study the history, the lifestyle and delve deeply into the furniture created by these gifted craftsmen. includes painstakingly detailed measured drawings of the original furniture pieces and hundreds of beautiful photos. learn the secrets of shaker construction while learning about the shaker's themselves.

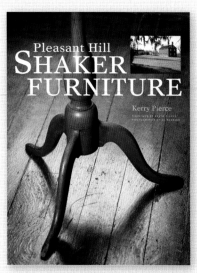

ISBN 13: 978-1-55870-795-5
ISBN 10: 1-55870-795-6
hardcover, 176 p., #Z0564

THE SMART WOMAN'S GUIDE TO HOMEBUILDING

By Dori Howard

Using the information in this book, you can:
• Improve your communication with homebuilding professionals
• Make informed decisions to keep you on schedule
• Get insider advice from experts in homebuilding
• Stay on budget and on time!

ISBN 13: 978-1-55870-817-4
ISBN 10: 1-55870-817-0
paperback, 160 p., #Z1027

POPULAR WOODWORKING'S ARTS & CRAFTS FURNITURE PROJECTS

This book offers a collection of twenty-five Arts & Crafts furniture projects for every room in your home. Some projects are accurate reproductions while others are loving adaptations of the style.

A bonus CD-ROM contains ten projects and ten technique articles to provide even more information on construction and finishing.

ISBN 13: 978-1-55870-846-4
ISBN 10: 1-55870-846-4
paperback, 128 p., #Z2115

AUTHENTIC SHAKER FURNITURE

by Kerry Pierce

The classic grace of the Shaker style is captured in twenty timeless furniture projects built using a combination of hand and power tools. With step-by-step photos and Pierce's clear instruction, you will discover how to build each unique creation, including:
• An armed rocker and a straight-back chair
• A drop-leaf table and a sewing desk
• Hanging boxes, bentwood boxes, clothes hangers and more!

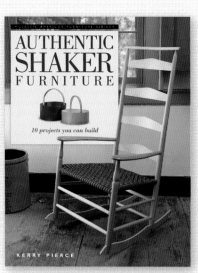

ISBN-13: 978-1-55870-657-6
ISBN-10: 1-55870-657-7
paperback, 128p, #70607

These and other great woodworking books are available at your local bookstore, woodworking stores, or from online suppliers.

www.popularwoodworking.com